LIFE SKILLS FOR TEENS AND YOUNG ADULTS

MONEY & CAREER EDITION; GAIN EMPOWERING, EXPERT ADVICE FOR A THRIVING FUTURE, FINANCIAL MASTERY & JOB SUCCESS WITH INQUISITIVE JOURNAL PROMPTS FOR PERSONAL CLARITY

ANNA B. JOELS

CONTENTS

Dear young readers, this book is for you.

To all the bright and talented young people out there who are destined to lead and change the world for the better. You are not just the future but also the present, and I know that you will make a difference in your own unique way. Remember that the world needs your brilliant ideas, your kindness, and your courage. Keep dreaming big, keep learning, keep growing, and never give up on your passions and beliefs. I believe in you, and I cannot wait to see what you will achieve.

Thank you for being a source of inspiration and hope, and may this book be a valuable resource on your journey toward success and fulfillment.

I would love to hear from you, comments, thoughts, ideas for future books etc.

Please email me at thegoodjujujournal@yahoo.com

BONUS CHAPTER

Hey there! I'm excited to announce that this book has an amazing free bonus chapter that is sure to knock your socks off! This chapter is about mastering the art of gracefully navigating through challenging dialogues and understanding their significance. So, if you're interested in learning about even more valuable skills that can help you build a successful and fulfilling life, then this bonus chapter is what you've been waiting for!

All of my books are like having a personal coach by your side, guiding you through life's challenges. I want you to have all the tools that will empower you to succeed, and that's why I've included this bonus chapter. So don't miss out on this valuable resource, and enjoy the extra knowledge and support!

Click the link Below:
https://bit.ly/BonuschapLSFT-MC

Scan the code below

INTRODUCTION

Are you a teenager or young adult who wants to master essential life skills to be successful in your personal, financial, and professional life? Are you worried about striking out on your own and navigating career and financial decisions? Well, you're not alone! Many young adults feel overwhelmed by the responsibility of making important decisions about their finances and career paths. There is a lot to know and sort out. In addition, many college graduates struggle to find employment in their desired fields, even with a degree. But don't worry; this book is here to help you navigate the money and career challenges of adulthood with confidence and clarity. It is the ultimate guide to building a strong foundation of life skills that will help you achieve your goals and financial success along the way. With tons of knowledge on managing your finances, choosing solid investments, getting that dream job, excelling in it, and then building a successful career and future, this book is your ultimate resource. So, let's dive in and start mastering your life today!

1

WHAT COMES AFTER SCHOOL, TRADE SCHOOL OR COLLEGE?

"Life is my college. May I graduate well, and earn some honors!"

— LOUISA MAY ALCOTT

As high school comes to a close, many young adults are left wondering what comes next. The options, from attending a trade school to heading straight into a career, can seem overwhelming. With so many choices and uncertainties, it's no wonder many teens feel lost in transitioning from high school to a career or further education.

This chapter aims to provide a comprehensive guide for navigating this important transitional period. From understanding the pros and cons of each educational path to exploring different career fields, readers will gain valuable insight into their options. Even those who choose to pursue higher education must decide between community colleges, four-year universities, and everything in between. We will delve into the financial side of post-high school life, including ways to pay for college and scholarships to help you ensure a successful financial future.

With the right skills and knowledge, young adults can confidently navigate the transition from high school and into the workforce or higher education. This chapter offers a roadmap for success that will undoubtedly prove invaluable for readers as they embark on this exciting new journey.

THE PROS AND CONS OF

Trade Schools

First of all, what the heck is a trade school, which can be also known as a vocational school/college or technical college? Trade schools provide specialized technical training to prepare students for specific careers. These schools offer a diverse range of programs in fields such as information technology, automotive training, nursing, and health sciences that generally range from 8 months to 2 years. Trade schools can be either public or private institutions, with many being run as for-profit businesses. The nature of trade school programs is designed to equip students with practical, hands-on skills and knowledge that are required to succeed in highly skilled jobs and careers. Upon completion of a program, graduates typically receive either a diploma or a trade certificate, both of which certify their acquired knowledge and preparedness to enter the workforce in their respective fields. Overall, trade schools can be an ideal alternative to traditional four-year colleges, particularly for those who aim to fast-track their careers, acquire specialized, in-demand skills, and enjoy job security in their chosen fields.

Pros:

- **Learn quicker:** Opportunity to acquire specialized skills in a shorter amount of time than traditional college
- **More one-on-one:** Smaller class sizes with more individualized attention from instructors and a more personalized educational journey
- **Hands on:** Immersive and hands-on training experience with a higher level of engagement and information retention.
- **Less expensive:** Financial benefits for those who cannot afford traditional college tuition.
- **Peace of mind:** Job stability and security in advantageous industries.
- **Focused use of time and money:** You are not learning skills that do not relate to your field, and not paying for classes you won't be using.
- **Convenience:** Has more convenient start dates and greater flexibility in course scheduling.

- **Help with finding a job:** Many offer job placement help.

Cons:

- **Costs more:** It's more costly than an apprenticeship.
- **Not a classroom setting:** You will miss the classroom social aspect (if that is your thing)
- **You need to vet the school:** Some may operate with the aim of generating profit rather than providing quality education. Make sure that they align with your goals and deliver on their promises.
- **Limited career growth:** Trade school typically only provides training and education for a specific skill or trade.
- **Limited school options:** There are fewer trade schools to choose from. This can make it difficult to find a school that offers the program you want, or one that is located near your home or work.
- **Limited financial aid options:** Many do not offer the same financial aid packages as traditional colleges. This can make it difficult for students to afford the cost of tuition, books, and other expenses.
- **Class competition:** Many students are competing for the same limited job opportunities, there can

be a sense of pressure and tension among
classmates.

- **Rigorous schedule:** Many times, students attend
  classes during the day and work at night or on
  weekends. This can be particularly challenging for
  those who are juggling other responsibilities.

Despite these potential drawbacks, there are many advantages to trade school and it can be an excellent option for those who are interested in pursuing a specific trade or skill. With the right training and education, graduates can go on to enjoy successful and fulfilling careers in a variety of industries.

> "The nature of trade school programs is designed to equip students with practical, hands-on skills and knowledge that are required to succeed in highly skilled jobs and careers."

COMMUNITY COLLEGES

Pros:

- **Cost-effective education:** Community colleges
  offer lower tuition fees compared to four-year
  colleges and universities. Students can save money
  on tuition fees and graduate with less student loan
  debt.

- **Flexible schedules:** Many community colleges offer evening, weekend, and online classes, making it convenient for students to balance work, family life, and education.
- **Opportunity to explore major options:** Community colleges offer a wide range of majors and courses, giving students the opportunity to explore their interests and career options before transferring to a four-year college or university.
- **Smaller class sizes:** With smaller class sizes, students can receive more personalized attention from their professors and have more opportunities to participate in class discussions and activities.
- **Qualified professors:** Community colleges employ experienced and qualified professors who are dedicated to teaching and helping students succeed. These professors often have real-world experience in their fields and can provide valuable insights and advice to students.
- **Transitional:** Community colleges offer a smooth transition from high school to college for students who are not yet ready for a four-year college or university.
- **Gives time to decide:** Earn college credit while taking your time to find the perfect four-year institution that fits your needs.
- **Close to home:** Community colleges are often located in or near students' hometowns, making it

easy for them to commute to class or live at home while attending school.

Cons:

• **Limited course offerings**: Community colleges may have a smaller selection of courses to choose from, limiting your academic experience and exposure to different fields of study.

• **Less prestigious degree**: Some employers may view a degree from a community college as less prestigious than one from a four-year university, which could impact job opportunities in the future.

• **Lower student engagement:** Due to the lighter workload and lack of campus life, students may not be as actively engaged in their studies or extracurricular activities.

• **Limited resources:** Community colleges may have fewer resources available such as research facilities, specialized equipment, and amenities that other colleges offer.

• **Transferring credits:** If you plan on transferring to a four-year university, not all of your credits may transfer, causing you to potentially lose academic progress and spend more money on additional courses.

• **Stigma:** Despite numerous successful alumni, there is still a stigma attached to attending a community college which can lead to feelings of self-doubt and questioning your academic abilities. However, it's important to remember that education is education, no matter where you receive it.

Overall, while community colleges offer a variety of benefits like lower tuition costs and more flexible scheduling, it's important to consider the potential drawbacks before making a decision. However, when taken advantage of correctly, a community college education can be just as valuable and beneficial to your future as one from a four-year university.

> "The swiftest way to triple your success is to double your investment in personal development."
>
> — ROBIN SHARMA

4 YEAR COLLEGE

Pros:

- **Wage increase:** A 4-year college degree increases your earning potential and job opportunities. On average, college graduates earn significantly more than those with only a high school diploma. In fact, according to the Bureau of Labor Statistics, individuals with a bachelor's degree earn more than double that of those with only a high school diploma.

- **Expanding your horizons:** College provides a unique opportunity to explore your interests and challenge yourself. You have access to a variety of resources and diverse perspectives that can expand your mind and shape your worldview.
- **Personal relationships:** Attending college allows you to build lasting personal and professional relationships. You will meet people from different backgrounds and cultures that can broaden your perspectives and help you grow as a person. I still have close friends that I met in college 40 years ago.
- **More than just a classroom:** Many colleges offer hands-on experiences, such as internships and research opportunities, that can provide valuable skills and connect you with professionals in your desired field.
- **Reduced sticker price:** While the upfront cost of college can be daunting, many students do not pay the full tuition. Scholarships, grants, and financial aid can significantly reduce the cost of attendance. It's worth visiting the admissions office of your potential college to inquire about available financial aid options to help cover the cost
- **Professional/mentoring relationships:** Professors and mentors offer guidance and support beyond the classroom, preparing students

not just for academics but also for the professional world.

- **Job requirements:** A college degree is required for many jobs, even in fields that were previously open to those with only a high school diploma. By obtaining a degree, you increase your chances of qualifying for a wider range of job opportunities and advancing in your career.

Cons:

- **Skyrocketing tuition:** This makes college expensive, and it may not be worth the investment.
- **Lower ROI:** College degrees are not yielding the return on investment that they used to. Many graduates do not find jobs related to their studies.
- **Lost income:** Students who attend college lose out on potential income during their college years. This can be a financial burden for many students.
- **Large debt:** Loans and debt can cripple college graduates, making it difficult for them to get ahead financially.
- **Not always a challenge:** College doesn't necessarily "grow" your mind. Many students are not challenged academically or given opportunities to explore new ideas.

- **Tough transition:** College does not necessarily prepare you for the real world. Many graduates struggle with the transition from college to career, as they are not prepared for the challenges they will face.
- **You may still lack skills:** College may not prepare students for the job market as well as they think. Some employers are looking for skills and experience that are not necessarily taught in college.
- **Different maturity levels:** Not all 18-year-olds are ready for college. Students may be better off taking a gap year or pursuing other opportunities before deciding to attend college.
- **Takes true effort:** Attending college without vigorously applying yourself won't magically sharpen your cognitive powers. Students who aren't willing to put in the effort will not necessarily benefit from the experience.
- **Time better spent:** The time and money spent on a college education could be better used on other endeavors, such as starting a business, pursuing a trade, or investing in personal development.

College can provide lasting relationships, hands-on experiences, and access to financial aid to reduce tuition costs. However, there are drawbacks such as skyrocketing tuition costs, lower return on investment (ROI), lost income, and large debt. It may not always challenge you or prepare you for the real world, and it may take true effort to get the most out of college. Ultimately, it's up to each individual to decide whether attending college is the right decision.

TYPES OF FINANCIAL AID

- **Grants:** This type of financial aid doesn't need to be repaid and is usually awarded based on financial need.
- **Loans:** Loans are borrowed funds that must be repaid after graduation. Federal loans typically have lower interest rates and more flexible repayment options than private loans.
- **Work-study jobs:** Through the Federal Work-Study program, eligible students can earn money for college expenses by working on campus or with approved off-campus organizations.
- **Scholarships:** Scholarships may be awarded based on academic achievement, athletic ability, artistic talent, leadership skills, community service, or other criteria. Many scholarships are merit-based, but some are based on your financial situation.
- **Aid from your college or career school:** Colleges and career schools may award institutional grants or scholarships based on factors such as academic achievement, financial need, or intended major.

- **Aid From Your State Government:** Most states offer financial aid programs for residents attending in-state colleges or universities.

State tuition-free education, here are the deets!

- Currently, 17 states in the United States offer some form of tuition-free college.
- These programs vary in terms of eligibility requirements and available funding.
- Some states, such as Tennessee and Oregon, offer free community college for all residents.
- Some programs, require students to maintain a certain GPA and attend college full-time to remain eligible.
- In some states, students are required to live and work in the state for a certain period of time after graduation in order to qualify for the program.
- Some states require students to complete community service or work-study programs as part of their eligibility.
- Tuition-free programs may be limited to certain degree programs or community colleges.
- Some states use a "last dollar" funding model, where other forms of financial aid must be applied first before tuition-free funds are awarded.
- These programs can help alleviate the burden of student loan debt for students and families.

- Keep in mind, that students are still responsible for other expenses like textbooks, room and board, and transportation.
- Some critics argue that these programs may not ultimately be sustainable or may not effectively target students with the greatest financial need.

Ways to find scholarships

- **Start early:** Begin your search for scholarships early in your high school career, ideally during your freshman year.
- **The more the merrier:** Apply to as many scholarships as possible.
- **Pay attention to details**: Make sure to follow all of the instructions specified by each scholarship's application.
- **Update yearly:** Keep your student profile updated annually to ensure that you are eligible for the most current scholarships available.
- **Some easier to get:** Merit-based scholarships are awarded based on academic or other achievements and are typically less competitive than need-based scholarships.
- **Shop local:** Local scholarships are a great starting point for your scholarship search but don't leave out national scholarships which can offer larger awards.

- **Small ones add up:** Be persistent in your search, as many smaller scholarships can add up to help you cover the cost of tuition and living expenses.
- **Use the web:** Use database search websites to help you locate national scholarships.
- **Don't stop once you start school:** You can even apply for scholarships while you're already in college and should do so throughout your college career.
- **First check with your school:** Check with your college's financial aid office to see if they offer any scholarships.

Scholarship search engines

Here are nine websites that can help you find scholarships you may be eligible for:

- **Scholarships.com:** This website has been around since 1998 and has assisted students in finding millions of scholarships based on their interests, academics, and skills.
- **Fastweb:** This website gives personalized scholarships that match the student's profile and interests.
- **Cappex:** Cappex has over $11 billion in scholarships listed on its website for students to apply. It assists students in finding scholarships

that meet their criteria, including GPA, test scores, and ethnicity.

- **Niche:** This search engine has a wide range of scholarships ranging from $500 to $2,000. It has over one million scholarships listed, and the website is user-friendly with a clear interface. Niche also provides student ratings and reviews on colleges and universities.
- **Chegg:** Chegg offers personalized scholarships based on the student's profile. Chegg also has partnership programs with various organizations, giving students more scholarship options.
- **Peterson's:** This website allows users to filter scholarships by academic level, field of study, and location.
- **Unigo:** This website has a college matching tool that helps students find a college or university that meets their preferences.
- **Scholly:** Scholly is an easy-to-use app that allows students to swipe through a list of personalized scholarships based on their profile.
- **ScholarshipOwl:** ScholarshipOwl has a streamlined, three-step application process that allows students to apply for multiple scholarships in just one application.

Finding scholarships can be overwhelming, but these scholarship websites and search engines make the process more manageable. Take advantage of these resources and increase your chances of winning a scholarship to help pay for college.

THE INS AND OUTS OF APPLYING FOR FINANCIAL AID

It's important to note that you may be eligible for multiple types of financial aid and should explore all your options before deciding how to pay for college. The Free Application for Federal Student Aid (FAFSA) is the first step in applying for most forms of financial aid.

• **Which ones do you need?** Research and decide which type of financial aid you need, grants, scholarships, loans, or work-study programs.

• **FAFSA:** Complete and submit the Free Application for Federal Student Aid (FAFSA) form, which is the most important financial aid application for prospective college students in the US. You can file online at the official FAFSA website or pick up a paper copy from your school's financial aid office.

• **What else do you need?** If you're applying for state financial aid, check if you need to complete any additional forms or documentation besides FAFSA. Also, keep in mind that many state financial aid programs have priority deadlines.

• **What are the individual requirements?** Many colleges and universities require a separate financial aid application along with the admissions application. Check with each school you're interested in to see what their specific requirements are.

• **Give yourself enough time:** There are deadlines for submitting all financial aid applications. It's a good idea to start the process early, so you have enough time to gather all the necessary paperwork.

• **Your financial documents:** Financial aid applications often require documentation such as tax returns, bank statements, and pay stubs.

• **Your SAR:** After you've submitted your FAFSA form, you'll receive a Student Aid Report (SAR), which will summarize the information you provided and contain your Expected Family Contribution (EFC).

• **Review it all:** If you receive a financial aid award letter, make sure you carefully review the terms and conditions of the aid package, including any loans you may need to repay. Consider the total cost of attendance, including tuition, fees, room and board, and other expenses, to avoid surprises.

• **Maintain eligibility:** Keep in mind that financial aid may be renewable or limited, based on certain factors. Make sure you understand the requirements and deadlines for maintaining your eligibility.

GAP YEAR

Taking a "gap" year between high school and college has become more popular in recent years as more students are looking for extra time to consider their future plans. While it may not be the right choice for everyone, it's important to consider all of the options available before making a decision about higher education. This year can be used to work and save money, travel, or gain work experience that can prove valuable in their future studies and careers. Research has shown that students who take a gap year often return to college with a clearer sense of purpose, more focused goals, and a readiness to succeed. In fact, many college admission officers see the gap year as a positive experience, as it can help students develop important skills such as independence, self-reflection, and cultural awareness. It's important to note, however, that a gap year should be well-planned and structured to ensure that it is productive and aligned with one's goals. With careful planning and a clear sense of direction, a gap year can be a rewarding experience that ultimately leads to greater success in college and beyond.

WEIGH THE PROS AND CONS AND DECIDE

The transition from high school to a career or further education is a crucial period in the lives of young adults. This chapter has provided a comprehensive guide for navigating this important transitional period, exploring various educational paths and career fields. It is important for readers to consider each option carefully and weigh the pros and cons using the information provided in this chapter. It will help them make informed decisions that align with their interests, goals, and aspirations. By doing so, they can position themselves for a successful and fulfilling future.

YOUNG PEOPLE CHANGING THE WORLD

There are so many incredible young people who have made such a positive change in the world. Their persistence, ingenuity, and compassion are truly inspiring. However, it can be easy to get caught up in the enormity of their accomplishments and forget about the power of individual actions. The truth is that we all have the ability to make a significant difference in the lives of others, no matter how simple our actions may seem. As you read this book, remember that you too have the ability to change the world – one act of kindness, one moment of bravery, and one small step at a time.

Billie Eilish

Billie Eilish is a fast-rising star in the music industry known for her unique voice. She is a brilliant artist that is way beyond her years. She started writing music at the age of 11 and has been wowing the world with her music ever since. She made her mark as an outstanding singer-songwriter, with her music resonating with audiences worldwide. Her debut album, When We All

Fall Asleep, Where Do We Go?, made history by winning five of the six prestigious Grammy nominations. While her earlier EP cemented her status as the youngest artist to earn a billion plays on Spotify. Her clever, intelligent, and fierce pop songs have lit up the musical charts, winning her numerous accolades and legions of fans. With her enigmatic personality and thought-provoking lyrics, Billie Eilish has become a cultural icon inspiring many on her musical journey.

Try this:

Go visit a college and sit in on a class. Do you like the vibe? How did it make you feel? Go to the cafeteria, do you like the atmosphere there? Did you feel like you belonged there?

A PLACE FOR MY THOUGHTS

This is a place to grab your journal and write your thoughts about the chapter or reflect on the provided prompts.

- Where do I want to be in five years. What do I want my life to look like?
- What path would be the best way for me to get There?

- Write out 10 pros and cons about your first choice for what you decide to do after school
- Write out 10 dream aspects of either the school you want to go to or the job you want to have.

Done with College.....Now What?

2

WHAT COMES AFTER SCHOOL, MILITARY?

"I am not a product of my circumstances. I am a product of my decisions."

— STEPHEN COVEY

Joining the Military is a decision that can have a lasting impact on a person's life, both professionally and personally. It involves a significant amount of dedication, hard work, commitment, sacrifice, and risk, but it also offers numerous rewards and opportunities. By serving in the armed forces, individuals can make a meaningful contribution to their country, gain access to benefits, receive a secure salary, and obtain valuable life skills. It is essential to weigh the pros and cons of joining the Military carefully. In this chapter, we will delve into the background context of the pros and cons of joining the Military, including the requirements for joining, the benefits and challenges, and what to know before making such a decision.

As someone who has grown up with a father and two brothers who served in the Military, I understand both the benefits and challenges of joining the Armed Forces. While on active duty, they were deployed to various countries, and I could see the toll that it took on them physically and mentally. Having them away from home for extended periods was tough, and I worried about their safety and well-being. However, now that they are retired from the Military, I can see the benefits of their service. They receive retirement pay, access to exclusive military clubs and resorts, and an extended "military family" wherever they go. They are in good shape physically and one brother now works in other countries using the knowledge he gained during his service. The Military has provided my brothers with a sense of purpose and pride, and they have formed lifelong friendships with people who share their experiences. While joining the Military comes with its own set of challenges, it can provide a fulfilling and rewarding experience for those committed to serving their country.

THE PROS AND CONS OF....

Joining the Military

Pros:

- **Like-minded friends for life:** You can forge lifelong friendships based on your unique experiences.
- **Experience new countries and cultures:** Gain a deeper appreciation for the world and learn how we are all connected.
- **Secure employment & salary:** You can be assured of job security for as long as you serve your country.
- **Access to benefits:** Depending on your rank, you can access various benefits such as support for rent payments, free healthcare, and additional days off.
- **Purpose and passion:** It is a way to make a meaningful contribution to society and have a sense of pride in your achievements.
- **Free education & impact on your well-being:** You can learn how to deal with stress, improve your skills, and even attend college.
- **Higher social status:** As part of this elite group, you are respected and admired for the service you provide to your country. Additional benefits that come with being part of this select group.

- **Preferred employee:** Former military personnel are preferred by business leaders for leadership roles due to their exceptional ability to strategize and solve problems even under high-pressure situations.

Cons:

- **Risks:** Joining the Military can be dangerous, as soldiers may be deployed to war-torn regions and face physical harm or even death.
- **Uncertainty:** When you sign up for the Military, you may not know where you'll be sent and what you'll be doing, which can lead to uncertainty and stress.
- **Away from home:** For those with families, joining the Military can be especially difficult because it means being away from loved ones for long periods of time
- **Worry:** Families of military personnel often worry about their loved one's safety and well-being.
- **Challenging:** Military life can make it challenging to plan for the future, as deployments and other assignments can disrupt career plans.
- **Less money:** While the Military provides compensation, joining is not a quick way to get rich, and soldiers typically make less than their civilian peers.

- **Possible injury:** Military training and service can lead to serious injuries, including traumatic brain injuries, amputations, and psychological scars.
- **Demanding:** The demands of military life can be grueling, including long and irregular hours, physical exertion, and mental stress.
- **Rules and orders:** When you join the Military, you may have to comply with rules and orders that you disagree with, even if they go against your personal beliefs or values.
- **Hard to get out once in:** There may be limited opportunities to quit once you've joined, meaning that you may be stuck in the Military even if you no longer want to be there.
- **Stress etc:** Many military personnel suffer from mental health issues, such as post-traumatic stress disorder (PTSD), depression, and anxiety, which can last long after their service ends.
- **Relationship strain:** Joining the Military can also mean being separated from friends and family for long periods, making it difficult to maintain relationships and social networks.

"It involves a significant amount of dedication, hard work, commitment, sacrifice, and risk, but it also offers numerous rewards and opportunities."

REQUIREMENTS FOR JOINING THE MILITARY

- **Age:** The minimum age to join the Military is 17 (with parental consent) or 18 without consent.
- **Education:** A high school diploma or equivalent is required for most military positions. Some positions may require additional education or specialized skills.
- **Physical fitness:** All military personnel must meet minimum physical fitness standards and maintain fitness throughout their service.
- **Citizenship:** In most cases, applicants must be United States citizens or legal permanent residents
- **Background check:** All applicants are subject to a background check, which may include criminal history, drug use, and financial background.
- **Medical exam:** All applicants must pass a medical examination to ensure they are physically and mentally fit for service.
- **ASVAB:** The Armed Services Vocational Aptitude Battery (ASVAB) is a test used to determine eligibility for military service and identify the best job fit for each individual.
- **Commitment:** The Military is a commitment, and service members are expected to be available for deployment at any time, depending on your chosen branch and job. It is important to

understand the level of commitment required before joining.

- **Basic training:** You will need to complete basic training, which is a rigorous program designed to prepare you for military service.

A COMMITMENT BUT REWARDING

Joining the Military is an opportunity to improve your life and the lives of those around you while enjoying job security and salary. It is a serious commitment that comes with both rewards and challenges. It is also a chance to meet like-minded people, travel the world, gain access to benefits, and find a purpose. You will also play a significant role in contributing to the security and welfare of one's country. If you're considering joining the Military, take the time to research your options and discover if it is the right fit for you.

Try this:

Talk with someone who just joined the Military and then speak to someone who is retired. Make a list of the questions you may have about the points in this chapter, and ask them what their answers would be. I also invite you to email me the same at thegoodjujujournal@yahoo.com. I'd love to hear from you.

YOUNG PEOPLE CHANGING THE WORLD

Kavya Kopparapu.

Kavya Kopparapu is the founder and CEO of Girls Computing League, an impressive nonprofit organization that has already impacted countless students across the world with its focus on teaching emerging technology. As an ambitious and driven individual, Kavya has been passionate about making a difference in the field of STEM from a young age. This has led her to create the first artificial intelligence conference for high school students, which has since become a hallmark event for aspiring young tech enthusiasts. Kavya's experiences of being the only student and one of the only women at research conferences and in the tech field has inspired her to ensure that students from diverse backgrounds and identities have access to the same opportunities, support, and resources to thrive in STEM. Her latest initiative to support students at colleges with limited resources to enhance participation, access, and readiness in emerging technology and computer science shows her commitment to the cause. Her vision and leadership have tremendously helped Girls Computing League become a significant player in the space, and her exceptional work continues to inspire future generations of girls in STEM.

A PLACE FOR MY THOUGHTS

- Am I the kind of person who would do well serving in the Military?
- What pros do I like about serving in the Military?
- What cons am I not okay with?
- What would it be like to serve overseas?
- Am I willing to leave my family for an extended period of time to go overseas?

3

JUMPING STRAIGHT INTO A CAREER

"Do the best you can in every task, no matter how unimportant it may seem at the time. No one learns more about a problem than the person at the bottom."

— SANDRA DAY O'CONNOR

For many individuals, attending a traditional four-year college may not be a good option due to financial constraints, personal circumstances, or preferences. The rising costs of college tuition, student loans, and the uncertainty of landing a job after graduation have caused many individuals to rethink the traditional path to success. However, this does not mean they cannot achieve their career goals. Instead, they can choose to explore a wide range of paths that are available to them. According to Fortune magazine, some lucrative careers do not require a college degree. Trades such as electricians, plumbers, and carpenters are in high demand, with many companies actively seeking out individuals who have skills instead of those with a traditional college education. The rise of online learning platforms and vocational schools has made it easier for individuals to obtain the necessary skills and certifications for a well-paying job in their chosen field. Therefore, it is essential to understand that there is no specific path to success, and one can attain one's career aspirations without following the traditional college route. In this chapter, we will explore the plethora of opportunities available outside of college and provide insights into how these paths can lead to a fulfilling career.

JUMPING RIGHT IN

Pros:

- **Avoid student loan debt:** You can start earning right away and save money by avoiding the financial burden of tuition, room and board, textbooks, and other college-related expenses.
- **Learn valuable skills:** You can benefit from on-the-job training and acquire practical skills that are in demand by many employers
- **College degrees are not always required:** Many industries don't require a degree, such as construction, transportation, and healthcare.

- **Experience is an asset:** Many employers value work experience over college degrees when hiring, promoting, or giving raises.
- **Less stress:** You can avoid academic pressures, exams, papers, and deadlines and focus on developing your professional potential instead.
- **Networking:** You can build a professional network of colleagues, mentors, and clients who can support and guide your career advancement.
- **Cuts to the chase:** You can jump into a career that aligns with your passion, interest, and goals rather than spending time going through a generic curriculum or major.
- **Your own boss:** You can become an entrepreneur without having to wait for a diploma or a certificate.
- **Take charge:** You can gain a sense of independence, responsibility, and confidence by taking control of your career path.
- **Tuition assistance:** Many employers will provide or help pay for self-development or college.
- **It does not have to be permanent:** You can always return to college or pursue further education later in life if you feel the need to enhance your skills, broaden your knowledge, or change your career path.
- **Gain perspective about education:** Working before college can lead to a greater appreciation

and understanding of the benefits of learning and can motivate students to excel in college.

- **Gain perspective about a career:** It's possible you'll like working so much more than being in school that you decide to forgo college altogether.

Cons:

- **Limited career opportunities:** Without a college degree, you may be restricted to entry-level jobs with limited growth potential.
- **Low earning potential:** Studies show that college graduates earn significantly more than high school graduates. By skipping college, you may miss out on reaching a higher income.
- **Missing out:** College years are typically a time for personal growth and self-discovery as you live independently, have access to diverse communities, interact with people from diverse backgrounds, and learn different perspectives on life.

THE HOW-TOS OF JUMPING RIGHT IN

Many successful individuals have taken a different route after high school and jumped right into their careers. Numerous opportunities are available for those who choose to enter the workforce immediately. In fact, with the right mindset, determination, and work ethic, you can build a thriving and fulfilling career without a college degree.

- **Explore your career aptitude:** Take online career aptitude tests to identify your interests, skills, and values to determine a suitable career match.
- **Consider certifications:** Earning industry-recognized certifications to increase your employability and demonstrate your expertise in your chosen field.
- **On-the-job training:** Some offer on-the-job training programs to gain valuable work experience and acquire new skills.
- **Internships or volunteer opportunities:** They can provide hands-on experience and a better understanding of your desired career path.
- **Take online courses:** Enhance your knowledge and skills by taking online courses related to your field.
- **Find a mentor:** Seek guidance and support from experienced professionals who can provide valuable advice.
- **Network:** Develop a network of professional contacts by attending events, joining industry associations, and connecting with professionals through social media platforms.

> "The rise of online learning platforms and vocational schools has made it easier for individuals to obtain the necessary skills and certifications for a well-paying job in their chosen field."

JOBS THAT DON'T REQUIRE A COLLEGE DEGREE

Although this is a short list, it will give you some idea of the types of jobs that are out there.

- **Electrician:** It typically takes four years of apprenticeship to become a licensed electrician, but you can quickly start your career by working as an electrician's helper.
- **Plumber:** To become licensed, you must complete classroom training and apprenticeship.
- **HVAC technician:** To get started in this field, you can enroll in a trade school program that typically takes two years or more.
- **Dental hygienist:** You can become a licensed dental hygienist by completing a community college or technical school program.
- **Sales representative:** You can apply directly for a sales rep job without prior knowledge or experience. Although, some research about the job will help you land one.

- **Web developer:** This job requires knowledge of programming languages such as HTML and CSS and can be self-taught or gained through online classes
- **Construction worker:** This can be self-taught or learned through classes.
- **Personal care aid:** You can become a personal care aide by completing a short training program.
- **Personal trainer:** This job requires that you be certified in cardiopulmonary resuscitation (CPR) and automated external defibrillator (AED). You will also need to complete an accredited course. This could be self-study online or attending a vocational school or college for more in-depth learning. Some gyms also offer in-person personal trainer courses.
- **Hairstylist:** Many states require you to complete a licensed cosmetology program.
- **Truck driver:** While you'll need to get your commercial driver's license, you can typically complete training in weeks.
- **Technical or computer support specialists:** You may be able to start out with just your high school diploma or GED and later take a computer training class. You may be required to later obtain certifications such as CompTIA A+, CompTIA Network+, and CompTIA Security+.

THE BEST OF BOTH WORLDS, APPRENTICESHIP

Apprenticeships have been around for centuries, and for good reason. They offer individuals a unique opportunity to develop practical skills and theoretical knowledge, all while getting paid. By combining classroom instruction with hands-on experience, apprenticeships provide a holistic learning experience that prepares individuals for well-paying careers in high-demand industries. According to the U.S. Department of Labor, participating in an apprenticeship program can increase earnings by an average of $300,000 over a lifetime. Not only that, but apprenticeships are also a vital tool for building a resilient and highly-skilled workforce. By bridging the gap between education and employment, apprenticeships ensure that individuals are equipped with the right skills and experience to succeed in their careers. With over 950 different apprenticeable occupations to choose from, there is no shortage of opportunities for those looking to embark on this exciting journey. So, whether you're interested in a career in a skilled trade or a high-tech industry, apprenticeships are an excellent way to learn, grow, and achieve your professional goals.

Degree apprenticeships

Degree apprenticeships are a fantastic option for those looking to gain a degree while also gaining valuable work experience. Not only do you earn a full undergraduate or master's degree, but you also get 3-6 years of on-the-job training and experience. This means that when you finish your degree, you'll have skills and experience that will make you an attractive candidate to future employers. And the best part is that you won't be saddled with the same level of debt as a traditional university student! Degree apprenticeships offer a flexible way to learn, with part-time university study that can be fitted around your work schedule. So, if you're looking for a way to gain a degree with less financial burden and more practical experience, a degree apprenticeship could be the perfect pathway for you.

HOW TO FIND ONE

Here are some steps you can follow in order to find and get an apprenticeship.

- **What type you are looking for?** It's important to identify what you want to do before you start your search.
- **Speak to a career advisor:** They can suggest different apprenticeships or provide further information to help you make an informed decision.
- **Check the entry requirements:** Apprenticeships have different entry requirements, which depend on the level of the apprenticeship. Generally, entry requirements are based on educational

qualifications, such as school grades, GCSEs, or A-levels.
- **Apply for the apprenticeship:** Be sure to read the application instructions carefully and complete all sections fully.
- **Attend the interview:** If you are invited for an interview, you can expect to be asked questions about your education, work experience, and motivation for pursuing the apprenticeship. Be prepared to answer questions thoughtfully and confidently.
- **Start the apprenticeship:** If you get the apprenticeship, congratulations! You will begin your training and work with your provider, employer, and mentor to achieve your goals.

CHALLENGING BUT REWARDING

Keep in mind that apprenticeships can be challenging, but they provide many opportunities for learning and growth, as well as the chance to gain valuable work experience.

SO MANY CHOICES, WHICH ROAD WILL YOU TAKE?

It is clearly evident that attending a traditional four-year college is not the only path to achieving a successful career. High costs, personal circumstances, preferences, and uncertainty associated with obtaining a degree need not limit you and have led many individuals to explore alternative options. Trades such as electricians, plumbers, and carpenters are becoming increasingly popular due to the high demand for skilled professionals, making it easy to obtain the necessary skills for a promising career. It is essential to understand that success is not limited to a degree, and alternative pathways can lead to a fulfilling and rewarding career. One can pave their unique path to seeking opportunities, achieving their goals, and success.

Try this:

After you know what trade you want to learn, find a school that teaches it online or in person. Visit it, and see what you think. Do you like the atmosphere, the vibe, and the feel of the place? Do you feel like you belong there and could thrive there?

YOUNG PEOPLE CHANGING THE WORLD

Malavika Kannan

Malavika Kannan is an inspiring young activist and writer who has significantly impacted the lives of girls and youth of color in America. Her journey began in middle school when she wrote the first draft of her book, which has now been published as The Bookweaver's Daughter. This powerful and empowering book features a young South Asian woman in a leading role. Alongside her accomplishments as a published author, Malavika founded the

Homegirl Project in 2018, an organization that started as an online magazine and has grown to empower girls and youth of color to become political leaders of tomorrow. While stepping down from the project to focus on her book release, Malavika continues to advocate for others and believes in paying it forward. Her message stresses the importance of using one's privilege and power to free and lift up others. Malavika's journey is an inspiring story of a young activist who continues to make a huge difference in the world.

A PLACE FOR MY THOUGHTS

- Which trade skills would I be interested in learning?
- Which pros and cons stand out for me between trade school and college?
- What job would make me the most fulfilled in my life (write as though anything is possible because, in fact, it is)?
- Is there an apprentice available for that career and would that be a good path for me to take?

4

FINDING A GOOD JOB

"If opportunity doesn't knock, build a door."

— MILTON BERLE

Transitioning from high school to the workforce can be a daunting task. After years of academic focus, it's time to venture into the world of work, which requires different skills and knowledge. Finding the right job is crucial in setting the foundation for a rewarding career, and it involves several essential steps. This chapter will guide you through the process of finding a good job that aligns with your interests, values, and career goals. From attending job fairs to job search platforms and networking, we will provide actionable tips and strategies to ensure you're well-prepared and confident in your search. Let's delve into the world of work and discover exciting opportunities that await you!

THINGS TO CONSIDER BEFORE YOU BEGIN (INCLUDING WHAT YOU WANT)

JOB FAIRS ARE GREAT FOR SEEING WHAT'S OUT THERE

Attending job fairs can be a proactive approach to job hunting, brimming with benefits for those who do it right. Job seekers are able to meet prospective employers with potential career opportunities face-to-face and showcase their skills and achievements. Making the most of these events is essential to creating a lasting impression and securing a possible job offer. Effectively leveraging these events requires preparation, self-confidence, and a few tricks. Below are some tips to help you get the most out of job fairs.

- **Take careful notes as you go:** Make sure you keep track of the name, and title of the person you spoke with, the company name, and any other contact information you may need, so the thank you and the follow ups are accurate.
- **Research beforehand:** Before heading to the job fair, gather information about participating companies and job openings to have a clear idea of their requirements and job descriptions. This research will assist you in deciding which employers to target, tailoring your resume, cover

letter, and pitch, creating questions to ask recruiters, and knowing what to expect during the event.

- **Prepare your marketing materials:** Bring several copies of your resume, and make sure it represents you well. Ensure your contact information is up to date. Also, create an introduction speech (your pitch) that will hook recruiters, highlight your qualifications, and present you as a viable candidate. This speech should take about 30 seconds. Make sure you practice beforehand.
- **Your appearance:** Portray a professional image and create a positive impression by sporting a clean, wrinkle-free outfit. A haircut and trim might not hurt either.
- **Mind your body language:** Your body language sends critical messages when interacting with employers. Aim to look confident, approachable, and engaged. Make eye contact with recruiters, give firm handshakes, and demonstrate an upbeat, positive attitude.
- **Have a plan:** Create a plan for the job fair that includes the companies you want to meet and the order of priority for meeting them. Arrive early and take advantage of the opportunity to get your bearings. Seek out your top choices first while you are fresh. This will also allow you to create another impression with them by visiting

again later in the day to thank them for their time.

- **Network with fellow attendees:** Job fairs provide unparalleled opportunities to network, learn about other job openings, and meet job seekers with similar qualifications. Don't be afraid to chat and exchange contacts with attendees you meet.
- **Follow up afterward:** It's crucial to follow up with the employers you've met within a day or two of the fair. Reach out to thank them for their time, inquire about the hiring process, and express your interest in the position. This polite act can help you stand out and make a lasting impression.

Attending job fairs is a critical part of any job search strategy and makes the most of your time and effort. Follow these essential tips, and soon you'll be well on your way to finding your dream job.

> "Making the most of these events is essential to creating a lasting impression and securing a possible job offer."

FOCUS ON MORE THAN JUST WHAT YOU'LL BE PAID

Finding the right job is a crucial decision that will significantly impact your life on a personal and professional level. When searching for a job, it's important to consider several factors to ensure you make the best choice that aligns with your values, career goals, and interests. Here is a comprehensive list of things you should consider when looking for a job to help you make an informed decision.

- **Company culture:** Look for a company that shares your values and has a positive work environment that you feel comfortable in. This will ensure that you feel fulfilled and engaged in your work.
- **Job responsibilities:** Make sure the responsibilities align with your interests and career goals. This will increase your chances of feeling challenged and engaged in your work.
- **Compensation and benefits:** Consider the company's salary and benefits package. Ensure it aligns with your financial expectations and provides healthcare, retirement plans, vacation time, and other relevant benefits.
- **Location:** Consider the location of the job and your commute time. The office location should be convenient and easy to access. If not, are you willing to do the extra traveling to get to work?
- **Colleagues:** Your colleagues can impact your work environment and job satisfaction. Finding a company where you enjoy working with your colleagues and feel like you are part of the team is crucial.

- **Technology:** The company should provide the necessary technology and tools to help you perform your work effectively. Check if they invest in technological advancements and offer training opportunities.
- **Recognition and appraisal:** Find out if the company provides regular feedback, recognition, and appraisal to keep you motivated and if they encourage and give opportunities for your career growth.
- **Flexibility:** The company should provide a flexible work culture that allows you to work from home or have flexible hours if needed.

Finding the right job that aligns with your needs and interests requires thorough research and careful consideration of the above factors. It's important to take the time to assess your priorities and ensure that the company you choose provides the necessary support, recognition, and opportunities for growth to help you achieve your career goals.

INTERNET AND JOB SEARCH PLATFORMS ARE USEFUL

USING JOB SEARCH ENGINES

Finding a job can be daunting, but with the right tools and strategies, it doesn't have to be. Job search engines are an excellent starting point, as they offer a wide range of job opportunities from various sources. Jobseekers can use these platforms to tailor their search criteria, receive job alerts, and access information about desired job positions and the companies providing them. Here are some useful tips for utilizing job search engines to maximize your job search success:

- **Start with job search aggregators:** Job search aggregator websites like Indeed and SimplyHired are great starting points when looking for job openings. These websites compile job listings from various sources, including company websites and job boards, to provide a comprehensive list of opportunities in one place. Be sure to upload your resume to these sites to make it easier for recruiters and employers to find you.
- **Add additional focused sites:** Depending on the desired industry or job position, specialized job websites may offer more specific job search options or access to industry-specific job listings.

For example, suppose you're looking for a job in the tech industry. In that case, you may consider using sites like Dice and GitHub Jobs, whereas Hcareers is designed for those seeking hospitality jobs.

- **Go mobile:** Many job search engines, such as Indeed and LinkedIn, have mobile applications that allow job seekers to access job listings, save job searches, and apply for positions directly from their phones. This is a convenient way to stay up-to-date with the latest job postings and quickly apply for positions. This can be especially helpful if you are actively employed or have a packed schedule.

- **Use advanced search features:** To narrow down your job search and find the most relevant job openings, make use of advanced search features. These features allow job seekers to specify the job location, job level, and desired salary to see only the jobs that meet their criteria.

- **Create job alerts:** Setting up job alerts is another way to stay informed about job opportunities. Job search engines allow job seekers to set up job alerts based on their job search criteria and receive notifications when new job openings that meet their criteria are posted. This saves job seekers time by eliminating the need to search for job listings manually.

By utilizing these tips, job seekers can streamline their job search process and increase their chances of finding relevant job openings that meet their criteria. Remember, it's essential to use job search engines strategically to achieve the best results. Happy job hunting!

IF YOU KNOW WHERE YOU WOULD LIKE TO WORK, CONTACT EMPLOYERS DIRECTLY

One of the most effective ways to secure a job interview is by contacting employers directly. Here are some valuable tips on how to contact an employer to apply for a job and follow up with them:

- **Tailor to the company:** Research the company before sending an application to understand its ethos, objectives, and culture better. This will help you tailor your application and show you're a good fit for the organization.
- **Quality letter:** Craft a well-written cover letter that introduces yourself. It should be personalized and demonstrate your qualifications for the specific job.
- **Make it relevant to the job:** Tailor your resume to the specific job you are applying for by emphasizing your relevant achievements and experiences.
- **Contact Leadership when possible:** When contacting the employer, connect with the hiring

manager or someone in a leadership position, if possible.

- **Be professional:** Use a professional email address and attach your resume and cover letter. In the email, introduce yourself and express your enthusiasm for the position.
- **No nickname emails:** I had a friend who was looking for a new job and did not get any bites until she changed her cutesy email to an email with just her name. She was hired for a job not long after that.
- **Keep in touch:** Follow up with a phone call to reiterate your interest in the role and inquire about the status of your application.
- **Be ok with waiting:** Be patient but persistent and gracious in your communication, as you may have to wait for a response.

If done correctly, contacting an employer directly can increase your chances of getting the job you want. Showcasing your interest, professionalism, and attention to detail could make a big difference in standing out among other qualified candidates.

USE YOUR NETWORK FOR JOB REFERRALS

When searching for a job, utilizing your network and seeking job referrals can significantly improve your chances of landing a position. Not only can your connections provide valuable insights and guidance, but they may also be able to recommend you for a job directly. Sometimes, that is all you need to land that job.

- **List your contacts:** Start by reaching out to your personal and professional contacts, such as teachers, Principals, guidance counselors, Clergy, coaches, bosses, friend's parents, and mentors. Let them know that you are actively seeking new opportunities and ask if they know of any positions that would be a good fit for you.
- **Use confidence:** Don't be afraid to ask for a referral. If one of your contacts knows of a job opening that interests you, ask if they would be willing to recommend you for the position.
- **Expand your reach:** Utilize social media to expand your network. Joining professional groups on LinkedIn or reaching out to alumni networks on Facebook can connect you with people who may be able to help with your job search.
- **Find new contacts:** Attend networking events and job fairs to meet new people who can provide job leads or referrals.
- **Thank and return the favor:** Be sure to thank your contacts for any help they provide and offer to return the favor in the future. Maintaining strong professional relationships can be beneficial throughout your career.

By employing these tips, you can leverage your network to increase your chances of finding job opportunities and receiving referrals.

ATTENDING BUSINESS NETWORKING AND FORMAL SOCIAL EVENTS

Business and social engagements can be daunting for some individuals. However, with the proper knowledge and etiquette, you can confidently navigate any event. From accepting invitations to making a memorable toast, this guide will provide you with the necessary skills to ensure that you leave a lasting impression.

- **Receiving invitations:** Carefully note the date, time, location, and dress code, if any. Then, RSVP promptly, either by the method specified on the invitation or by a polite email or phone call, expressing your appreciation for the invitation and your intention to attend or regretfully decline. It's recommended to respond within 24 to 48 hours of receiving the invitation. If you're unable to attend, be sure to give a valid reason, but keep it concise and positive.
- **Proper attire:** Dressing appropriately for the event is a sign of respect for the host and shows that you take the occasion seriously. For a business event, it's always better to go for formal or semi-formal attire. Men should opt for a well-

tailored suit, shirt, and tie, while women can choose from formal dresses or power suits. It's important to dress for a social event based on location, theme, and occasion. However, it is also essential to be comfortable and confident in your attire to enjoy the event to the fullest.

- **Hello, goodbye, and the talk in between:** Start by introducing yourself to the host and then others by engaging in conversation while being respectful of their time and opinions. Express interest in what they say and actively listen to their stories. Show your appreciation by thanking the hosts and organizers for putting on a successful event. Make sure you don't forget to mention any speakers or presenters who have made an impact on you.

- **When and how to make a memorable toast:** Knowing how to make a toast graciously and effectively can set you apart from others. Consider the timing of the toast. It's best to wait until everyone has settled and is ready to listen attentively. Make sure to speak from the heart and be authentic. Share an anecdote or a personal story that is relevant to the occasion. Use thoughtful language, but don't be afraid to inject some humor or lightness to keep the mood upbeat. Lastly, keep it short and sweet. A truly memorable toast is one that everyone can remember and cherish without it dragging on.

By following these tips and practicing etiquette, attending formal and business events can become less intimidating. Remember, your behavior reflects not only on you but also on your organization or company. By showing respect and appreciation to the host, you are building relationships that can lead to future success. So, go forth and confidently conquer your next formal event!

BRAND YOURSELF ON SOCIAL MEDIA

In today's digital age, it is more important than ever to be able to present yourself professionally online. Social media has become an essential tool for many of us, whether job hunting, networking, or just connecting with friends and family. However, it's crucial to keep in mind that everything we post online contributes to our personal brand. In other words, our social media presence can make or break our professional reputation. To do it successfully, here are some things to consider:

- **Use your real name:** This may seem obvious, but using a pseudonym can make it challenging for people to find and connect with you. And most of the time, it looks less professional.
- **Get everything squeaky clean:** Go through your past posts and reviews online and delete anything that can put you in a bad light. Potential employers can see anything that is public on your profile.

- **Be consistent:** Use the same profile picture, cover photo, and bio across all social media accounts.
- **Get your personal branding down:** Know what message you want to convey to the world. In a few sentences, summarize who you are, your skills, and what makes you stand out. Use this statement on your social media profiles and in your job search materials (the same as your pitch but a bit shorter).
- **Show your stuff:** Use social media to showcase your portfolio or blog, and curate posts that influence and highlight your expertise.
- **Bring all your accounts together in one place:** Use platforms such as Linktree or About. Me as a jumping-off point to centralize your social media accounts and include it in your job search materials. Making it easy for them to learn about you will increase the chances that they will.
- **Don't use it for professional communications:** Avoid communicating sensitive or confidential information on social media. Instead, use more secure platforms such as email or phone calls to communicate professionally.
- **Use scheduling tools to stay on top of things:** Use apps like Hootsuite to manage your social media accounts more efficiently and schedule posts ahead of time.

BRANDING YOURSELF ON LINKEDIN

- **Optimize your profile:** Create an impressive profile that showcases your skills, experience, and education. Filling out the experience and education sections with relevant keywords will help you rank higher in search results.
- **Use a professional profile picture:** Your profile picture is the first thing people see when they visit your profile. Make sure you use a professional-looking photo that aligns with your industry.
- **Craft a compelling headline:** Your headline should be a short and snappy description of what you do, whom you serve, and how you help.
- **In the about section:** Use this section to tell a compelling story about your professional journey, achievements, and future aspirations. Keep it concise yet compelling.
- **Showcase your skills and expertise:** List your skills and expertise and get endorsements from your colleagues and industry peers. This helps build credibility and enhances your professional reputation.
- **Keep your profile up-to-date:** Update your job title and responsibilities, education, certifications, and any other relevant information regularly so that your profile reflects your current skills and expertise.

- **Participate in groups**: Join industry-specific groups and engage in conversations with like-minded professionals. This is a great way to demonstrate your knowledge, build relationships, and make new connections.
- **Publish content:** Share your knowledge and expertise by publishing articles and blogs. This helps you position yourself as a thought leader and increases your visibility.
- **Network strategically:** Reach out to people in your network who are relevant to your industry, profession, or career goals. Be clear about why you are reaching out and what you hope to accomplish, but also be respectful and mindful of their time.
- **Reconnect with old contacts:** Think about former colleagues, clients, or classmates whom you may have lost touch with over the years. Reach out to them with a quick note or connection request and see if there are any opportunities to collaborate.
- **Engage:** Keep in touch with your connections by commenting on their posts, sharing their content, and personalizing your messages. This helps build relationships and keeps you on top of their mind.
- **Keep under the radar:** If you're looking for a new job, make sure you keep your search under the radar by turning off the "Notify your network?" section in your LinkedIn settings.

By following these LinkedIn branding tips, you can create a powerful online presence, build your professional network, and attract new career opportunities.

> "In other words, our social media presence can make or break our professional reputation."

BRANDING YOURSELF ON FACEBOOK

Keep it professional: First and foremost, it's important to be mindful of the information you're sharing on your Facebook profile. You don't want to give potential employers a reason to doubt your professionalism.

- **No fear:** Don't be afraid to showcase your personality and interests on your Facebook profile. This can help you stand out among other candidates and connect with like-minded individuals. Just make sure you do so in a respectful and appropriate manner.
- **Update often:** Use your Facebook profile to share professional updates, such as articles about your industry or news about your latest project. This shows that you're passionate about your work and keeps you at the top of their mind for potential job opportunities.
- **Engagement:** engage with companies and organizations aligning with your brand and

professional goals. This can be done by "liking" their pages and sharing their content. It shows that you're informed and interested in your field.

- **Let them know:** consider letting your Facebook connections know if you're currently searching for job opportunities. This can be done through a status update or a message to your most trusted connections. You never know who may have a lead for you!

TWITTER

- **Be consistent and creative:** Tweet regularly and focus on quality over quantity. Share a mix of curated content, industry news, and your own insights. Make sure to add value to the conversation and show off your expertise.
- **Engage:** Engage with your followers by responding to their tweets, retweeting their content, and asking questions. This helps to build relationships and expand your network.
- **Hashtag correctly:** Use relevant hashtags to increase visibility and attract new followers. Research industry-specific hashtags and join Twitter chats to connect with like-minded professionals.
- **Be you:** Don't be afraid to show your personality on Twitter. Share a behind-the-scenes look at

your day-to-day work, respond to trending topics, and inject humor into your tweets.

- **Keep up on the latest:** Follow other thought leaders and major players in your field to stay up-to-date on industry trends and connect with potential mentors.
- **Get organized and keep track:** Create lists of interesting people to follow, such as industry influencers or potential job leads. This will help you stay organized and engage with the right people.
- **A tool to keep in touch:** Use Twitter to complement your in-person networking efforts. Follow up with new contacts on social media and continue the conversation online.

Remember to be authentic and true to your brand on Twitter. Don't try to be someone you're not, and don't sacrifice your values for social media success.

ITS MORE OF A PROFESSIONAL TOOL THAN YOU THINK

Creating a strong personal brand on social media is essential in today's professional world. It takes a lot of effort and commitment, but with these tips, you can build a polished online presence that will help you stand out from the crowd. The image you project online can significantly impact your career, so be sure to invest your time in strategizing and presenting yourself effectively.

Try This:

Do you know someone who owns a business? If you do, ask them to give you a practice interview.

Ask a trusted friend to give you feedback on your social profile. Does it look professional enough? What changes would they suggest?

Make plans to attend a job fair and attend it (even if you are afraid to do it).

YOUNG PEOPLE CHANGING THE WORLD

Anne Frank

Anne Frank was a Jewish girl born on June 12, 1929, in Frankfurt, Germany. When she was four, her family moved to Amsterdam to escape the impending Nazi persecution. However, the occupation of the Netherlands by the Nazis in 1940 soon caught up with them. In the summer of 1942, the Franks went into hiding in a secret annex behind Otto Frank's business premises along with four other Jews. During this period, Anne kept a diary chronicling her thoughts, emotions, and experiences of living in hiding. Unfortunately, the Gestapo discovered their hiding place in August 1944, and the family was deported to the Auschwitz concentration camp in Poland.

Anne and her sister Margot were later transferred to the Bergen-Belsen concentration camp, where they lost their lives. Despite her untimely death, Anne Frank's legacy lives on through her diary, which has been translated into numerous languages and continues to inspire and educate people around the world about the horrors of war and discrimination.

The story of Anne Frank resonates with me at a deeply personal level. I am Polish and a descendant of those who lived through the horrors of Nazi occupation. There were more Polish people killed during the Holocaust than any other group.

A PLACE FOR MY THOUGHTS

- What fears do you have about entering the job force?
- Are those fears really true? What evidence do you have that makes them true?
- What is your first choice for places to work? Why?
- Pick one of the listed questions that an interviewer may ask you and thoroughly answer it

5

GETTING THE JOB AND BEING HAPPY WHILE YOU ARE THERE

"Find out what you like doing best, and get someone to pay you for doing it."

— KATHARINE WHITEHORN

Getting a job as a teenager can be really overwhelming. It is understandable to feel uneasy about putting yourself out in the job market and facing intimidating figures such as job ads, cover letters, letters of intent, and interviews. It can also be an exciting opportunity to learn new skills, gain independence, and build your resume. However, it is essential to remember that getting a job is just the beginning. What you do while you are there is just as important, if not more so, in shaping your future education and career prospects. In this chapter, we will discuss some essential aspects of getting a job and being happy while you are there, including how to prepare for an interview, how to build confidence when starting a new role, and how important team culture is within the job. With these tools in hand, you will be ready to take on whatever job opportunities come your way and make the most of it.

LETTER OF INTENT

Are you looking for a job that matches your skills and experience, but no suitable opportunities are currently available at your dream company? A letter of intent, also known as a letter of interest, may be just what you need. This letter allows you to express your interest in working for a certain company and highlight your professional accomplishments. It can also give you a chance to reconnect with a recruiter you've met at an event. If you want to stand out among other potential candidates, a letter of intent can demonstrate your passion and dedication to the field and the specific company.

Two letters, the difference

A letter of intent should not be confused with a cover letter, which is used to apply for a job and is to be included with your application.

Letter of intent: When a job is not available but you are really interested in working for a particular company. This is to show them your intention for wanting to work for them someday. This is to show interest to the company in general.

Cover letter: This "covers" your job application. This is used as an introduction to you when submitting a job opening that you would like to fill. This is specific to the job that you are seeking.

How to write one

- **Tailor it to the company:** Research the company beforehand (tips on how to do this are in the next section) and use that knowledge to tailor your letter to their needs and goals. This will show the employer that you're serious about the position and have taken the time to get to know their organization.
- **Be professional:** Use a professional font and format the letter like a business letter. This includes including a header, salutation, body paragraphs, closing, and signature.
- **Make a connection:** Start with a strong opening paragraph that grabs the reader's attention. Use a personal reason or experience to create a human connection right from the start.
- **Show your best stuff:** Wow the employer with your accomplishments and expertise. Use specific examples and metrics to demonstrate your skills and experience.

- **State your reason:** Address why you want to work for this specific company. This shows that you've done your research and are genuinely interested in the company and its mission.
- **Ask for the next step:** Close with a call to action, such as asking for an interview or offering to follow up with additional materials.
- **Be picking about grammar:** Proofread the letter several times for spelling and grammar errors. Ask someone to run through it for you also.
- **Don't stop at the letter:** Follow up with the employer after sending the letter to demonstrate your enthusiasm and interest.

By following these steps, you'll be on your way to crafting a powerful letter that will set you apart from other job applicants.

Interview skills

Don't go in blind–research the company

Researching a company before an interview is a crucial step towards securing your dream job. It helps you understand the organization's values, goals and operations, and enables you to ask intelligent questions that showcase your interest and enthusiasm for the role. Here is how you can conduct effective company research before attending an interview:

- **Social media:** Check out the company's social media accounts, such as Twitter, Facebook, and LinkedIn, to get a sense of how they interact with their customers and partners. Note down any recent events, news, or updates that the company has shared on social media.

- **Online sources:** Begin by reviewing the company's website, paying close attention to its About Us, Mission, and Values pages. This will give you a clear understanding of the organization's mission, goals, and overall philosophy.

- **Finances:** Research the company's financial health by reviewing their annual report, which contains financial statements such as balance sheets, income statements, and cash flow statements. You can also use financial sites like Yahoo Finance or Google Finance to find out more about the company's revenue, stock price, and market position.

- **Their blog etc.:** Take some time to read the company blog and any other publications or press releases. This will give you a sense of the company culture, its leadership style, and the types of projects and initiatives that the company is currently focusing on.

- **Their competitors:** Conduct competitor research to understand the company's position in the marketplace. Look at other companies in the same industry or sector to identify potential threats and opportunities. Pay attention to how the company positions itself against its competitors, and why it stands out from the crowd.

- **Your questions:** Prepare a list of questions that you can ask in the interview. These should be based on your research and should show that you have taken the time to understand the company. They can be about the company's culture, recent projects, upcoming initiatives, or any other relevant topic.

By conducting effective research before an interview, you'll be able to demonstrate your knowledge and enthusiasm for the company. You'll also be better prepared to answer questions and discuss your fit for the role. Remember to approach your research with a curious, open mindset and avoid making assumptions about the company.

Practice with common interview questions

They are going to ask them, might as well be prepared, you may want to check the web for additional potential questions.

- **Tell me about yourself:** Create your elevator speech, highlight your relevant experience and skills, as well as your career goals and passions, in a short paragraph (the time of an elevator ride with someone). Be concise and professional, but don't be afraid to inject some personality and enthusiasm. They want to know what sets you apart from everyone else. Practice, practice. practice before hand!

- **Why do you want to work for this company?** Do some research and find out what sets this company apart from others in the industry. Highlight any values or initiatives that align with your own values and career goals.
- **How did you hear about this job?** Be honest and specific about where you found the job posting whether it was through a job board, social media, or a referral from a friend or colleague.
- **Tell me about something on your resume**: Choose a specific accomplishment or experience that demonstrates a skill or quality the hiring manager is looking for. Be specific and give details.
- **Why are you looking for a job?** Be honest and positive and professional - perhaps you're looking to expand your skill set, work in a different company culture, or pursue a new career direction.
- **Where do you see yourself in five years?** Highlight your career goals and aspirations, but be realistic and adaptable. Show that you're

committed to learning and growing, and open to new opportunities and challenges.

- **Why should we hire you?** Be confident in your skills, experience, and qualifications that make you a valuable addition to the company. Use specific examples and show your enthusiasm for the job.
- **Tell me about a conflict you faced at work and how you dealt with it**: Be honest, positive and professional, and focus on how you successfully resolved the conflict and learned from the experience. Be specific and give details.
- **What is your dream job?** Highlight your passions and career goals, but be realistic about how this job fits into your overall career trajectory. Show your enthusiasm for the job at hand, even if it may not be your "dream job."
- **What do you expect out of your team/co-workers?** Show that you value and respect collaboration, teamwork and diversity in the workplace. Emphasize how you communicate and work effectively. Be specific about what you expect in terms of communication, accountability, and support.
- **What do you expect from your manager?** Show that you value clear expectations and communication from your manager, and Emphasize your desire for feedback, growth,

support. and guidance. Be specific about what you expect in terms of leadership.

- **How do you deal with stress?** Be honest and specific about how you cope with stress, whether it's through self-care, time management, or seeking support from others. Highlight any skills or strategies that help you stay focused and productive under pressure.

- **What would the first 30 days in this position look like for you?** Show that you're organized and proactive, and talk about how you would prioritize your tasks and get up to speed quickly. Be specific about any questions or concerns you have at the outset, and show that you're eager to hit the ground running.

- **What are your salary requirements?** Be honest but flexible, and research similar roles and salaries in your industry and geographic location. Highlight your value as a candidate, but also be open to negotiation and other forms of compensation.

- **Do you have any questions?** Be prepared to ask thoughtful questions that demonstrate your interest in the company and the role. Ask about company culture, goals for the position, and are opportunities for growth and development.

Are there reasons the interviewer might doubt you? Are you the right one for the job?

It's important to remember that during an interview, an interviewer is trying to determine if you're the right fit for the position. If you lack certain skills or experience, they may doubt your ability to effectively perform the duties. They may question whether you have the necessary knowledge and expertise to complete tasks efficiently and accurately. In some cases, they may feel that your lack of experience will pose a risk to the team or company. It's important to address these concerns by highlighting your strengths, demonstrating a willingness to learn, and providing examples of times when you've successfully tackled similar challenges. Ultimately, your attitude and eagerness to grow can be just as important as your current skill set.

Employment gaps

When you have employment gaps on your resume, it's important to be ready to justify them in an interview. This is because it can suggest that you lack commitment or have been unable to secure work. However, there are many valid reasons why someone may have gaps in their work history, such as personal illness, caring responsibilities, further education, or taking time out to travel. It's important to be honest about your reasons for any gaps and to highlight any skills or experiences you have gained during that time. Remember that everyone's career path is unique, and a good interviewer should be understanding and supportive of your situation. Focus on highlighting your strengths and the value you can bring to the role, rather than dwelling on any gaps in your employment history.

When you have too much experience for the job

When an interviewer realizes that you have too much experience for the role, they may start to doubt your intentions for applying. They may question whether you will be satisfied with the position or whether you will quickly become bored and leave. They want to ensure that they are investing their time and resources in the right candidate or if the job is merely a temporary fix while you search for another opportunity. Additionally, they may wonder if you will be overqualified for the position, which could lead to some friction with your team members. By demonstrating your interest in the position and making it clear that you are committed to the role for the long haul, you can ease their concerns. By being open and transparent about your reasons for wanting to take a step back or make a career change, you can instill trust and help the interviewer understand that you are passionate about the position, regardless of your experience level.

If you lack confidence

An interviewer may doubt you if you appear nervous or lacking in confidence. They may worry that you aren't sufficiently qualified for the job. If you are unable to effectively communicate your skills and experience, the interviewer may wonder if you are embellishing them. If you are too anxious to articulate your thoughts, they may worry that you might not be able to communicate effectively with colleagues or clients and work well within a team. They may also question your ability to handle stressful situations, as many jobs require a degree of resilience. A lack of confidence may suggest that you don't believe in your own abilities, which could be a red flag for future performance issues. It's important for you to take the time to prepare thoroughly beforehand to alleviate your nerves and be able to present yourself in the best light possible.

To get that confidence going during an interview

Dress and punctuality: Dress professionally and arrive on time for the interview. Showing up late or looking disheveled can negatively impact your first impression.

Do your homework: Prepare thoroughly before the interview by researching the company, reviewing your resume, and practicing your answers to common interview questions.

Positive attitude: Show enthusiasm for the job and the company by highlighting why you're excited about the opportunity. Share previous experiences that make you a good fit for the position.

Body language: Nonverbal cues such as posture, facial expressions, and eye contact can convey confidence and professionalism. Sit up straight, maintain eye contact, and nod your head to show engagement.

Show interest: Maintain eye contact with the interviewer throughout the conversation. This will show that you're engaged and interested in the discussion.

Articulation: Speak clearly and confidently. Avoid using filler words like um or uh, and speak at a steady pace that is easy to understand.

Show knowledge: Demonstrate your knowledge and expertise by discussing past successes and accomplishments relevant to the position you're applying for.

Focus a bit on the company: Ask thoughtful questions about the company and the job to show that you're interested, engaged, and knowledgeable about the company.

Feedback: After answering a question, actively listen to the interviewer's response and be open to feedback. Acknowledge their comments to demonstrate your interest in their feedback.

Be yourself: Remember to stay calm, be yourself, and trust in your abilities.

Acknowledgment: Thank the interviewer for their time and express enthusiasm for the opportunity after the interview.

KEY POINTS TO KEEP IN MIND WHEN FOLLOWING UP

- **Timing:** Send your thank-you email within 24 hours of the interview. This will help you stay top of mind with the hiring manager and show your promptness and professionalism.
- **Content:** Take the extra effort and craft a well-written message that reiterates your enthusiasm. Be gracious and appreciative, but also confident and assertive in outlining why you are a good fit for the role. Briefly mention relevant skills and experiences, and sets the stage for any potential follow-up
- **Format:** Keep your email brief and easy to read. Use a professional tone and avoid any spelling or grammatical errors. Make sure to include your contact information and any additional materials (such as a portfolio or references) that were requested during the interview.
- **Follow-up:** If you don't hear back from the hiring manager within a week or so, send a brief follow-up message to inquire about the status of your application. This will show your persistence and interest, but try not to be pushy or aggressive. Remember that the hiring process can take time, and it's important to be patient and respectful throughout.

QUESTIONS THAT YOU SHOULD ASK

As a candidate for a new job, it is essential to demonstrate not only your skills and qualifications but also your commitment to contributing to the growth and success of the organization. Asking the right questions during a job interview can help you communicate your interest in the company's success and show your ability to think critically about the role. Here are some key questions to ask during the interview process that will demonstrate your enthusiasm for the position and your willingness to invest in the company's goals.

- As I begin my role, what objectives should I prioritize within the first 30 days in order to ensure I am contributing to the company's growth and success?
- What essential qualities and skills can I embody to excel in this role and contribute to the success of the company?
- How can I continuously work towards improving those skills?
- Could you please elaborate on how this position has evolved over the years, and how you see it continuing to develop in the future?
- What has turnover in the position generally been like?

- Can you describe the company's culture and values in detail, and how it has influenced the growth and success of the organization?
- Where do you envision the company heading in the next 5 to 10 years, and how do you plan on achieving those goals?
- Who are your main competitors, and what unique abilities can I bring to the table to help you surpass them?
- What do you anticipate will be the most challenging aspect of this position, and how can I prepare myself to meet those challenges?
- What are the current biggest challenges that the company is facing, and how can I contribute to overcoming those obstacles?
- What is your proudest achievement as a company thus far, and how can I contribute to continuing that success?
- What kind of training and support can I expect to receive as I begin my role, and how can I continue to develop and improve my skills?
- Can you describe the values and expectations that the company places on its employees, and how can I contribute to upholding those standards?
- What do you personally find motivating and fulfilling about working for this company?
- Have there been any successful strategies or approaches that past employees have taken in this

role, and how can I build on those successes and make it my own?

- Who will I be reporting to, and what can I expect in terms of communication and feedback with the company?
- Are there opportunities for growth and advancement within the company, and what kind of qualifications and contributions does it take to achieve those goals?
- Is there anything further I can provide or expand upon to better showcase my qualifications and suitability for this role?

The questions listed above will give you a well-rounded understanding of the company's culture, values, goals, and challenges, as well as provide you with an opportunity to showcase your qualifications and contribute to the company's progress. By asking these questions, you will increase your chances of securing the position and will be well on your way to contributing to the success of the organization.

QUESTIONS THAT YOU SHOULD NOT ASK

In an interview, it is important to be mindful of the questions that you ask. Asking inappropriate or irrelevant questions can leave a negative impression on the interviewer and affect your chances of getting the job. Here are some types of questions that you should avoid asking in an interview:

- Personal questions
- Questions about the company's finances
- Questions about the interviewer's political or religious beliefs
- Questions about salary and benefits that are not related to the job
- Questions about time off that are not related to the job
- Questions about the interviewer's personal life
- Questions that indicate your lack of research about the company or industry
- Questions that put the interviewer in an uncomfortable or awkward position
- Questions that reveal your intentions to leave the company soon
- Questions that are not relevant to the position you are applying for.
- Remember, the goal of an interview is to show your interest in the job and the company, as well as to demonstrate your qualifications and skills. By asking thoughtful and relevant questions, you can show that you are the right fit for the position.

> "As a candidate for a new job, it is essential to demonstrate not only your skills and qualifications but also your commitment to contributing to the growth and success of the organization."

Team culture, what it is, and why it is a good thing

Team culture is the foundation of any successful organization. When a team culture is strong and positive, it can have a massive impact on employee engagement, productivity, and satisfaction.

What is Team Culture?

Team culture refers to the values, norms, beliefs, and behaviors that are exhibited by the members of a team.

- It is the collective way of doing things that reflects the team's shared identity and purpose.
- A positive team culture creates a supportive environment where individuals can thrive and work effectively with others.
- It encourages open communication, collaboration, mutual respect and a shared vision that helps in achieving organizational goals.

Team culture sets the tone for the work environment, ensuring that each member is treated with respect and dignity. It is shaped by a combination of the team's leadership, communication, and employee engagement efforts, and is influenced by external factors such as industry trends and competition.

The Impact of a Strong Team Culture

A strong team culture results in engaged workers who are committed to the organization's success.

- It reduces interpersonal conflicts and facilitates effective communication between team members, leading to fewer misunderstandings and less stress.
- A positive team culture fosters creativity and innovation, as individuals feel empowered to offer ideas and perspectives that can drive growth and improve outcomes.
- It increases employee satisfaction and retention rates, reducing turnover costs and improving team cohesion.
- A strong team culture creates a great place to work, boosting employee morale and productivity.

Team culture is a vital component of any successful organization. It is not just about having a set of shared values but about creating a supportive, collaborative environment where individuals can thrive and work effectively together. This has numerous benefits, including improved employee engagement, productivity, satisfaction, and retention rates. Therefore, teams must focus on developing and maintaining a culture that supports their shared goals and values, where every member feels heard, appreciated, and respected.

Try This:

Write a practice letter of intent, and have a trusted mentor or friend read it, and give you feedback. Make sure they know that you are relying on their honesty, and when they are honest, thank them and consider and learn from their feedback.

YOUNG PEOPLE CHANGING THE WORLD

Gabriela Nguena Jones

Gabriela Nguena Jones is an inspiring and ambitious young woman who founded Teens Tutor Teens, a non-profit organization with a mission to bridge educational gaps and promote academic success amongst young people. She has partnered with GlobalGiving and secured grants from major corporations to fund her organization, which has already made a significant impact in the lives of many young people. Gabriela's leadership has been instrumental in the success of Teens Tutor Teens, as she has trained academically successful youth to mentor and tutor their peers who come from a less fortunate background. Her ability to manage and organize the operations of

Teens Tutor Teens while being a college student is commendable. Gabriela's resilience, grit, and determination to succeed have led her to overcome various challenges, including being told that she could not achieve her goals as a 16-year-old. Gabriela serves as a role model for young people who aspire to find their life's purpose and make a meaningful impact in their communities.

A PLACE FOR MY THOUGHTS

- What kind of company do I want to work in?
- What would keep me happy while I was there?
- What are the strengths I have that I could bring to a company?
- Pick one of the listed questions that an interviewer may ask you and thoroughly answer it.

Your Chance to Pay It Forward

"Together, we can change the world, one good deed at a time."

— RON HALL

Adulthood is just around the corner, and every new piece of information you soak up makes you better prepared for it.

My goal in writing this book was to make the transition into the world of money and career a little smoother for you. Armed with this essential knowledge, you'll gain the confidence to explore both yourself and the world around you, knowing that you possess all the tools necessary to tackle new financial responsibilities with ease.

By leaving a review of this book on Amazon, you'll show other teenagers where they can find the information they need to help them get there.

Thank you for your help with this. Being a teenager isn't simple, and I'm so happy you're up for making it a little easier for someone else.

Reach out to me at thegoodjujujournal@yahoo.com. I'd love to hear how you liked the book.

Did you get value from Life Skills for Teens and Young Adults: Money & Career Edition? Check out the first in the series, Life Skills for Teens and Young Adults: Health edition here:

Scan the QR code below to leave your review on Amazon.

6

REMEMBER, WORK ISN'T
EVERYTHING

"It is not the mountain we conquer, but ourselves."

— EDMUND HILLARY

Maintaining a good work/life balance is essential to leading a fulfilling and healthy life, yet it's become increasingly challenging to achieve in today's fast-paced society. In recent years, many people have fallen into the trap of prioritizing work over everything else, even at the expense of their well-being. This unhealthy work-centric lifestyle can lead to burnout, stress, and physical illness. That's why it's crucial to establish a good work/life balance early on in life before it is too late.

WAYS TO MAINTAIN WORK/LIFE BALANCE

Achieving a healthy work-life balance involves a combination of strategies and approaches that promote optimal well-being. Here are some key elements that can support you in achieving a healthy work-life balance

Setting Boundaries

- Establish a firm line between work and personal life by setting specific working hours that allow you to focus solely on work during specified times.
- Practice saying "no" to extra work if it extends into personal time or disrupts your work-life balance.
- Use calendars or time-management apps to prioritize work-related tasks, assign deadlines, and track progress.
- Create a dedicated workspace separate from the rest of your home, where you can concentrate and minimize distractions.
- Take regular breaks during the day to recharge, rest, and rejuvenate.

Time Management

- Schedule time for personal pursuits, such as hobbies, sports, or socializing, and make them a priority.
- Use your most productive time of the day to handle more challenging tasks and projects.
- Be realistic about your workload and set achievable goals to avoid feeling overwhelmed.
- Learn to delegate tasks that can be done by others so that you can focus on more critical tasks.
- Avoid multitasking, which can actually decrease productivity.

Stress Management:

- Practice mindfulness techniques, such as deep breathing or meditation, to help you relax and focus.
- Engage in regular physical activity, such as yoga or jogging, which can help reduce stress and improve overall wellness.
- Take regular breaks throughout the workday to prevent burnout and help you stay focused.
- Prioritize self-care practices, such as getting enough sleep, practicing mindfulness, eating a balanced diet, spending time with loved ones, and doing activities you enjoy.

- Don't hesitate to seek professional help when needed, such as counseling or therapy, to cope with stress and anxiety.
- Seek support from colleagues, friends, or family members when feeling overwhelmed or stressed.

Flexibility:

- Recognize that life is unpredictable, and be prepared to adjust your schedule and priorities when unexpected events occur.
- Look for ways to be more flexible in your work, such as adjusting your work hours or working from home.
- Learn to let go of perfectionism and acknowledge that a healthy work-life balance may require making sacrifices, such as declining invitations to work-related events or meetings outside of working hours.
- Manage your time effectively to allocate enough time for work, personal pursuits, and unplanned events.
- Be open to adapting to new technologies and processes that can help streamline work and improve flexibility.

> *"The future belongs to those who believe in the beauty of their dreams."*
>
> — ELEANOR ROOSEVELT

UNPLUG FROM WORK

How to "Unplug" From Work: Tips for a Healthy Work/Life Balance

Unplugging from work is crucial for maintaining a good work-life balance and overall well-being. Here are some ideas on how to do it effectively

- **Set clear boundaries**: Establish specific hours for work and stick to them as much as possible. Communicate your availability to your colleagues and clients so they know when they can expect to hear from you.
- **Plan your workload:** Prioritize your tasks and schedule your day ahead so you can focus on the most important ones first. Avoid overloading yourself with work right before you are supposed to finish, as it will make it harder to unplug.
- **Engage in physical activity:** Exercise is a great way to relieve stress, clear your mind, and boost your energy levels. You don't have to do anything intense; just move your body in a way that feels good.

- **Practice mindfulness:** Mindfulness is about being present in the moment and fully engaged in what you are doing. Take a few minutes to meditate, breathe deeply, or simply sit quietly and observe your surroundings.
- **Connect with others:** Spending time with loved ones, friends, or colleagues who share your interests can help you feel more relaxed and connected. Set up a virtual happy hour, or plan a picnic with friends to reconnect and have fun.
- **Pursue non-work-related activities:** Take a walk, read a book, or watch a movie you want to see. Find something that brings you joy and allows you to escape from the stress of work.
- **Take breaks throughout the day:** It's essential to take breaks during the workday to recharge your batteries and prevent burnout. Get up, move around, and do something that doesn't involve work for at least 10-15 minutes.
- **Set up a relaxing environment:** Create a calming atmosphere in your home or workspace with comfortable furniture, soothing music, and soft lighting. Make it a place where you can feel peaceful and relaxed.

Remember that unplugging from work is a process, and it may take some time to adjust to it. Be patient with yourself, and celebrate small victories along the way. With the right mindset, support, and strategies, you can successfully unplug from work and cultivate a more balanced life.

FINDING A JOB THAT YOU LOVE

When you love what you do for work, it truly doesn't feel like work at all. This is because you're genuinely passionate about what you do and you enjoy doing it. Being happy in your job is essential to your overall sense of well-being, as it can have a significant impact on your mental and physical health. Not only does loving what you do make you feel fulfilled, but it also often leads to better job performance and increased productivity. When you're passionate about your work, you're more likely to put in extra effort, take, and find creative solutions to challenges. In turn, this can result in greater job satisfaction, career advancement opportunities, and even higher salaries. Ultimately, if you have the chance to pursue a career that you're passionate about, jump in and take it - the rewards are truly immeasurable.

> "This unhealthy work-centric lifestyle can lead to burnout, stress, and physical illness. That's why it's crucial to establish a good work/life balance early on in life before it is too late."

Hobbies are not just goofing around

- Having a hobby has several health benefits. It can help you balance your work and life by giving you a sense of purpose and fulfillment outside of work.
- It can help us recharge and boost our energy levels, sharpen our skills, discover new talents, and make us more productive and creative at work.
- A hobby that aligns with your employer's culture can also improve your chances of getting a job or being promoted. For instance, participating in a golf outing for business can help create meaningful connections with colleagues and clients, leading to better opportunities.
- It can be a great way to meet new people and socialize. Being part of a group with similar interests can promote a sense of belongingness and foster new relationships.
- I have several friends who are newly retired and are having trouble because they spent so much of their time and energy at work and are at a loss for what to do with themselves in their later years.

Why it is so important to take vacations

It is imperative sometimes to take an extended break and recharge. That's where vacations come in. Planning a vacation can do wonders for our mental and physical health.

Why vacations are essential

- Vacations offer a break from the monotony of daily life, allowing us to recharge, catch up on sleep, and come back feeling refreshed and energized.
- They decrease stress levels, which can lead to better overall health and productivity.
- Vacations can help us gain new perspectives by experiencing different cultures and customs.
- Taking a break from work can increase productivity and creativity when we return.
- Vacations provide the opportunity to spend quality time with family and friends, create cherished memories, and strengthen bonds.
- They allow us to disconnect from technology and the constant demands of modern life.
- Vacations can improve our physical health by providing time for exercise, outdoor activities, and relaxation.
- They offer the chance to try new things and step outside our comfort zone.
- Taking vacations can improve our mental health by reducing anxiety and depression symptoms.
- They give us the chance to explore our interests and hobbies.

Vacations are more than just a luxury; they are essential to our mental and physical well-being. Vacations offer many benefits that can improve our overall quality of life. Whether it's a long weekend or an extended trip, taking time away from the hustle and bustle of daily life is always worth it. So take that well-deserved break and return feeling refreshed and ready to take on the world.

Other ways to make time for yourself and loved ones

Taking some time for yourself and your loved ones is crucial for your mental and emotional well-being. It helps you recharge your batteries and come back refreshed and ready to tackle life's challenges. However, with life's busy schedule, it can be difficult to prioritize 'me-time' and quality time with loved ones. Let's explore various ways to make time for yourself and your loved ones.

- **Plan a weekend getaway:** It doesn't have to be extravagant or expensive. A change of scenery can be an excellent way to refresh your mind and strengthen your relationship with loved ones.
- **Find a hobby together:** Hobbies are great for relieving stress and enjoying your free time. It could be anything from reading, painting, or baking.
- **Schedule a technology-free hour:** Disconnect from your phone, computer, and social media, and spend time with yourself or loved ones. It's a great

way to clear your mind and strengthen relationships with loved ones.

- **Go on a walk:** Walking is an excellent form of exercise and can be a great way to spend time with loved ones while also enjoying nature.
- **Spend quality time with your pet:** Pets can be great stress-busters and help you enjoy your free time. Take your furry friend for a walk, cuddle on the couch, or play a game of catch together.
- **Cook a meal together:** Cooking with loved ones can be a fun way to spend time together while also enjoying good food.
- **Take a day off:** Sometimes, a simple day off can do wonders for your mental health. Take a day to relax and recharge without any obligations or appointments.
- **Journaling:** Writing can be therapeutic and can help you express your feelings and emotions. It's a great way to have time and connect with yourself. You can also share not-so-private parts of your journal with your loved ones, such as your dreams and aspirations or a great idea you have come up with.

Making time for yourself and your loved ones is essential for your mental and emotional well-being. By trying some of the methods mentioned above, you can make time for yourself and your loved ones and enjoy a healthier, happier life.

Remember that achieving a healthy work-life balance is an ongoing, dynamic process that requires conscious effort and adjustment. By implementing these strategies and prioritizing your well-being, you can create a more fulfilling, less stressful life that supports your overall happiness and success.

> "Your work is going to fill a large part of your life, and the only way to be truly satisfied is to do what you believe is great work. And the only way to do great work is to love what you do."
>
> — STEVE JOBS

Finding your path can be easy with the right information

After-school decisions can be tricky, but they don't need to be if you take the time to weigh the options and consider what works best for you. My five kids all made different choices, and they're all doing well and happy with where they are. Two went to college, one went to trade school, and two entered the job market right after school. There's no right or wrong answer – it all depends on your interests and lifestyle. The important thing is to consider all your options and pick the path that is most comfortable for you. And if you need help making the decision, know that you have a supportive community around you.

YOUNG PEOPLE CHANGING THE WORLD

Louis Braille

Louis Braille was a Frenchman born in 1809 who was once able to see, but a devastating infection caused him to lose his sight at the tender age of five. He had a thirst for knowledge, and with the support of his family, he attended the Royal Institution for Blind Youth in Paris. Here, he learned about night writing, a system designed to help soldiers read messages without disclosing their location by lighting a torch. However, this system was complex and impractical. Fueled by his passion for learning and his deep-rooted empathy for his fellow blind students, Braille spent years refining a new tactile system of writing. By the time he was a young man, he had developed an innovative and practical system of writing that is still in use today, making communication more accessible for the visually impaired population worldwide.

Try this:

Interview two people you know who have gone straight into the job force and decided to start college later.

Create your "You time" ritual and schedule it into your calendar to help you unplug from work.

A PLACE FOR MY THOUGHTS

- How would I handle it if I was working too many hours and my boss asked me to work overtime onthe weekends?
- What would a balanced work/ life look like to me?

7

UNDERSTANDING MONEY MANAGEMENT

"Money, like emotions, is something you must control to keep your life on the right track."

— NATASHA MUNSON

MONEY MATTERS, BECAUSE MONEY MATTERS

Managing your money isn't just a basic life skill; it's crucial. Money is essential for survival and shapes many aspects of our lives, from the opportunities we can pursue to the quality of life we can lead. Effective money management can help us build wealth, achieve our goals, and navigate any financial hardship that comes our way.

This chapter will explore why money matters and the key aspects of effective money management. We will examine the role of money in modern society, the consequences of poor financial habits, and the benefits of sound financial practices. Furthermore, we will discuss what it means to manage your money effectively, including budgeting, saving, investing, and protecting your assets.

We will also delve into the impact of different economic conditions, such as inflation, interest rates, and market fluctuations, on your finances and how to prepare for them. By developing a comprehensive understanding of money management principles and practices, you can gain confidence and control over your financial situation, regardless of your current financial standing.

The good news is that it's never too late to start managing your money more effectively. Whether you're just starting out in your career, nearing retirement, or somewhere in between, this chapter offers valuable insights and practical advice to help you make the most of your money.

WHY IS MONEY MANAGEMENT IMPORTANT?

What is money management?

Money management entails managing your finances for optimum results. It involves a myriad of processes, such as budgeting, saving, investing, spending, and monitoring every penny you own, thereby ensuring that you don't overspend or live beyond your means. A well-organized money management plan can help individuals preserve their financial health and achieve future monetary goals. With better money management skills, you can save more, avoid debt traps, and plan for your long-term financial future. Ultimately, it boils down to making informed choices, setting financial goals, and being disciplined in your actions.

Why it is important

It is imperative for teens and young adults to learn money management; the earlier they start, the better. With a solid foundation in money management, they will be able to develop good habits that will serve them well for the rest of their lives. Poor money management skills can result in negative outcomes such as debt, bankruptcy, and financial insecurity. These can impact their mental health and relationships negatively. On the other hand, with proper money management education, financial stability can lead to reduced stress and improved mental and physical health. It allows for more opportunities and possibilities in the future, such as buying a house, starting a business, or investing in stocks. Knowing how to analyze financial risks and make informed financial decisions is also essential for anyone who wants to succeed in the business world. By learning money management at an early age, young adults can gain a head start on the path to financial security, obtaining the goals they have set, and ultimately, personal fulfillment.

Why goal setting is important

Understanding the importance of setting financial goals at a young age is crucial. It can help you achieve your dreams, whether buying your own home, traveling the world, or simply living comfortably without worrying about money. Without them, it can be easy to fall into a pattern of overspending and living paycheck to paycheck. By setting financial goals, you create an actionable plan to reach your desired financial state. It also helps to develop self-discipline and financial literacy, allowing you to make informed and responsible decisions about your money. Starting early also means you have more time to save and invest, allowing for greater financial success in the long run. So, don't underestimate the importance of setting financial goals. With hard work, dedication, and a solid plan, achieving a bright financial future is possible.

Apps to make it all easier

It can be challenging to stay on top of everything, especially when keeping track of all your expenses. Fortunately, there are numerous apps out there that can help make this task much more manageable. From budget trackers to banking apps, many options are designed explicitly to help you keep track of your finances. Some apps even offer features like reminders for bill payments, goal-setting tools, and personalized recommendations based on your spending habits. With easy-to-use interfaces and robust capabilities, these apps can help you create a realistic, achievable budget and take steps towards a more secure financial future. Whether you're looking to save up for a big purchase or simply want to reduce expenses and better allocate your resources, using a finance app can help you achieve your financial goals. So why not give one a shot today and see how much easier it can be to manage your money?

Automatic payments work even while you sleep

Automatic payments are arguably one of the most convenient, game-changing tools in the modern world. The fact that they work tirelessly in the background, regardless of what we are doing, is a true testament to their efficiency. Automatic payments can be a lifesaver for busy individuals who often find themselves strapped for time. Not only do they relieve the stress of remembering and manually paying bills, but they also prevent the accrual of late fees that can sneak up unexpectedly. The peace of mind that comes with knowing your bills are being paid on time is invaluable. Setting up automatic payments can truly feel like having your own personal secretary - always looking out for your best interests and keeping your finances in check. The best part is that once they're set up, you can truly "set it and forget it ."Having personally used this tool for years, I can confidently say that automatic payments have made my life infinitely easier.

Are Checkbooks Still a Thing?

The answer to this might surprise you. While the use of checks has reduced over time, checkbooks are still a viable alternative to make payments. There are situations where checks are the preferred payment method, such as rent payments or paying a freelancer. Moreover, many older adults still rely on checks to manage their finances. Although mobile banking has taken over, checkbooks are still a significant part of personal finance in the United States. Furthermore, check usage has remained steady in some industries, such as insurance and healthcare. Checkbooks are also needed for issuing foreign currency as well as to provide a legal record of payment. Despite the evolution of digital payment methods, checkbooks are still a practical and necessary tool in today's financial landscape.

What is a checkbook, and why it matters?

A checkbook is a powerful tool that gives you the ease and convenience of making financial transactions. With a checkbook, you can effortlessly pay bills or make purchases using the money in your checking account. It's a compact, paper-based pad, and every page contains a preprinted check with your name, address, and financial institution information. Each paper check in the pad is a legal document that represents an agreement to pay a certain amount of money to the payee. Checkbooks offer additional benefits such as preprinted deposit slips, which you can use to deposit cash or checks you have received. It is worth noting that many banks now offer online check depositing services, allowing you to deposit your checks from the comfort of your home. A checkbook remains one of the most reliable means of managing your finances, enabling you to stay in control of your spending and keep track of your transactions at the same time.

How to write a check

Writing a check may seem like an archaic task, but it's still a necessary skill in today's world. It is easier than you may think and best to learn before the time comes to write one.

- **Fill in the date:** Write the date in the top right-hand corner of the check. Be sure to write the full date, including the month, day, and year.
- **Write the recipient's name:** Write the name of the person or organization you're paying on the line that says "Pay to the order of." Make sure to spell their name correctly!
- **Write the payment amount:** Write the amount you're paying in numerical form in the box on the right-hand side of the check. Then, write out the amount in words on the line below. Make sure the amounts match!
- **Memo line:** If there's a specific reason for the payment, like rent or a donation, you can fill in the memo line at the bottom left-hand corner of the check.

- **Sign the check:** Finally, sign your name on the line at the bottom right-hand corner of the check. This is important – without a signature, the check is invalid.
- **Keep a record:** Make sure to write down the check number, amount, and payee in your check register for accurate bookkeeping.

It is a skill that takes a bit of practice. But once you get the hang of it, you can confidently and conveniently pay bills and make purchases using paper checks.

Why you should balance your checkbook.

Balancing your checkbook every month is a crucial habit that you cannot afford to ignore. This is especially true today, where fraudulent activities are on the rise, and banking errors can still occur. By being proactive and regularly reconciling your account, you can quickly spot any discrepancies and address them before they escalate into bigger problems. Additionally, by keeping a close eye on your transactions, you can monitor your cash flow and even discover ways to reduce your expenses. This practice can also help you achieve your savings goals by minimizing banking fees and increasing your savings on a regular basis. With the simplicity of online banking, balancing your checkbook has never been easier or more effective. So why wait? Start the habit of balancing your checkbook every month today and enjoy the peace of mind that comes with having a clear financial picture.

How do you do it?

Here's a step-by-step guide to help you balance your checkbook with ease:

- **Record interest earned:** In your checkbook register, make sure to record any interest earned on your account, as shown on your statement. This will add to your balance.
- **Record service charges:** Similarly, note down any charges on your account, such as monthly services, ATM transactions, etc. These will subtract from your balance.
- **Verify deposit amounts:** Check that all deposits listed in your register match the amounts on your statement. Make a list of any missing deposits to add to your balance.
- **Match check entries**: Match the entries in your register with the transactions listed on your statement. If they match, place a checkmark next to the transaction in both your register and on the statement. If they don't match, circle the item in both places so you can return to fix the error later.
- **Correct errors:** If there are any discrepancies, don't panic. Check your canceled checks, deposit receipts, and ATM receipts to identify and correct the error.
- **Check for outstanding items**: Make sure that all outstanding items (checks you wrote to someone

that has not yet been cashed) from previous statements have been included in the current one.

- **List outstanding checks:** Make a list of any outstanding checks or ATM transactions that have not been marked off in your register.
- **Verify other debits:** Confirm that all other debit transactions on your statement match the exact amounts you drew, such as ATM withdrawals or automatic payments.
- **Balance your checkbook:** Add up the ending balance on your statement, deposits not listed, and interest earned. Then, subtract all outstanding checks and service charges. Your total should match the ending balance in your register.
- **Online purchases:** Don't forget to include deductions from online purchases in your check register and indicate the transaction type. Note the transaction as an online purchase to differentiate it from paper checks. You can write the word "online" in the check number spot.

By following these simple steps each month, you can easily balance your checkbook and keep track of your finances. Don't forget to review your statements carefully to catch any errors or unauthorized transactions, and stay on top of your account to avoid overdraft fees or missed payments.

"Effective money management can help us build wealth, achieve our goals, and navigate any financial hardship that comes our way."

How in a paperless world?

In today's increasingly digital world, managing a checking account can be done more efficiently and conveniently than ever before. With the rise of electronic transactions, paperless statements, and mobile banking apps, tracking your spending and monitoring your account has never been easier. In fact, many banks now offer personalized budgeting tools and spending trackers integrated directly into their mobile apps, making it simple to keep your finances organized and on track. And with the added convenience of digital deposits and online bill payments, managing your checking account has never been more seamless. When I was a young adult, there was only one option: paper and pencil. I now do everything online and rarely visit my bank.

ELECTRONIC PAYMENTS

Electronic payments have become an increasingly popular mode of financial transactions in recent years. With apps like Apple Pay, PayPal, Zelle, and Venmo, consumers have more options than ever before to pay for goods and services conveniently and securely. According to a report by eMarketer, the total value of mobile payment transactions in the US reached almost $100 billion in 2019, and it is expected to continue growing rapidly. One of the benefits of using these platforms is that they offer an additional layer of security compared to traditional methods of payment. For example, many electronic payment apps use encryption technology to protect users' financial information. You can opt-in to be notified when a transaction is initiated. If you get this notification and it was not you who made the transaction, call your bank as soon as you can and let them know. It is smart to be proactive in helping to keep your accounts safe.

These apps also allow for quick and easy peer-to-peer payments, making them ideal for splitting bills or paying rent. Plus, by keeping track of purchases made through these apps, consumers can more easily manage their finances, budget accordingly, and seamlessly transfer funds without the need for paper checks or visits to the bank. All of these factors make electronic payments a convenient, accessible, and secure way to make financial transactions.

Alerts help you rest easy

Using checking account automation, notifications, and alerts can be a game-changer when it comes to managing your finances.

Automating regular payments and transfers can help you ensure that you never miss a payment and avoid late fees, keep your bills under control, and ease the stress of having to remember multiple due dates no matter how busy your schedule. Setting up reminders for low-balance alerts, loan payment deadlines, and even large purchases can help you stay on top of your finances and avoid potentially costly mistakes. From low balance alerts to fraud detection notifications, countless options are available to help you streamline your finances and make the most of your money. I have a notification sent to my email whenever there is a purchase of more than $100.00 on my checking or credit card accounts. If It is not a charge that I made, I contact my bank immediately. Being aware of what is going on in your account helps you address it before it becomes a major issue. Take control of your finances and enjoy greater peace of mind.

Start your money life out right

Effective money management is a fundamental life skill that can make a huge difference in our lives. Money is an essential aspect of modern society that impacts everything from our opportunities to our quality of life. Poor financial habits can lead to dire consequences, such as debt, poverty, and even bankruptcy. On the other hand, sound financial practices can help us build wealth, achieve our dreams, overcome money challenges, and maintain financial stability. Managing money effectively involves budgeting, saving, and investing. Developing a comprehensive understanding of money management principles and practices can give us confidence and control over our financial situation, regardless of our current financial standing. By embracing the key aspects of effective money management, we can achieve financial security, peace of mind, and a brighter future.

YOUNG PEOPLE CHANGING THE WORLD

Anvitha Kollipara

Anvitha Kollipara, a remarkable 15-year-old girl from Hyderabad, India, is the founder of the CareGood Foundation, a non-profit organization dedicated to giving voice to homeless senior citizens. Not only does she document their valuable stories and lessons on her blog, but she also provides them with much-needed emotional support. Her organization has set up immunity camps in old age homes and offers monthly medicine to 230+ senior citizens. Kollipara has also expanded her humanitarian vision to include solar power in the mission of the CareGood Foundation. She has provided over 700 rural children with solar-powered lamps and raised awareness about the importance of solar power and its positive impact on the environment. Her passion for helping others was nurtured through volunteering in public parks, gardens, orphanages, schools, and old age homes from a young age. Her inspiring journey and selfless service is a beacon of hope and a call to action for young people to find their life purpose and make a difference in the world.

Try this:

For the next month, write down every penny you spend to get an idea of where your money goes and how you need to budget.

A PLACE FOR MY THOUGHTS

- What are your biggest fears or challenges around money?
- What kind of life do you want to have during your retirement years?
- Were you surprised at where your money went when you wrote everything down that you spent this month?
- Are there places you need to increase spending or decrease it?

8

BUDGETING WILL HELP YOU REACH GOALS

"If it scares you, it might be a good thing to try."

— SETH GODIN

WHAT IS A BUDGET?

A personal budget is a financial plan that helps individuals track their income and expenses, providing a clear picture of their financial situation. It is a tool that allows you to decide how much money you want to allocate to each expense category while helping you save for the future and achieve your financial goals. Personal budgeting is especially important because it encourages people to develop a healthy relationship with money, which is crucial for economic well-being. Moreover, creating a budget can reduce stress and increase financial security, enabling you to prepare for unexpected expenses and emergencies. By managing your finances through budgeting, you can make informed financial decisions, avoid debt and overspending, and work towards a stable and prosperous future.

What to include in your budget

Creating a budget may sound daunting, but it's actually a straightforward process. Here are some must-have items to include in your budget:

Needs:

- Housing expenses (mortgage/rent, insurance, property tax)
- Transportation costs (car payment, gas, maintenance, insurance, public transportation)
- Health care expenses (insurance, medical costs)
- Utilities (electricity, natural gas, water, internet, phone)
- Groceries and household items
- Childcare expenses (if applicable)
- Minimum loan payments (student loans, credit cards, alimony, child support, etc.)
- Life insurance

Wants:

- Dining out and entertainment expenses
- Travel expenses

- Gym or club memberships
- Clothing and accessories
- Home decor
- Self-care treats like spa visits and pedicures

Savings and Debt Repayment:

- Emergency fund
- Retirement savings (401(k), IRA, other investments)
- Other investments
- High-interest debt repayment (credit cards, payday loans)
- Credit card payments
- Extra payments on a mortgage
- Extra payments on student loans

Different types of budgets:

Zero-Based Budget

Zero-based budgeting is a revolutionary technique used by companies that is also gaining popularity for personal budgeting. This method involves scrutinizing and analyzing every single expense from a starting point of zero. This means that every function within an organization is carefully assessed for its needs and costs, with no previous budgets acting as a baseline. With this technique, budgets are built around the exact needs for each upcoming period. The approach helps to identify and eliminate unnecessary expenses, making it an incredibly effective way for managers and individuals alike to optimize their budgeting processes. While it is undoubtedly more time-intensive than other budgeting methods, the thoroughness of this approach ensures that every penny is accounted for, making it a highly effective technique for financial management.

Pay-Yourself-First Budget

The pay-yourself-first budget is a smart and effective way to prioritize your savings and meet your financial goals. Treating your savings like a bill that must be paid first ensures you're putting money aside for your future before anything else. This budgeting method is easy to manage because it doesn't require you to track every single expense - as long as you're meeting your savings goals and not overspending, you're doing it right. Plus, by automating your savings with automatic transfers, you can set it and forget it, ensuring that your savings grow without any extra effort on your part.

Envelope Budget

With the envelope system, budgeting becomes a more straightforward and intentional process. To start, take some time to think about the different categories where you spend your money, such as groceries, dining out, or transportation. Then, decide on a specific amount of money you want to allocate toward each category. Label envelopes accordingly and fill them with the cash you have designated for each one. Whenever you make a purchase, use funds from the corresponding envelope and keep track of what you have spent.

One of the primary benefits of the envelope system is that it gives you a clear picture of where your money is going and helps you prioritize your spending. By addressing your needs, wants, and savings goals, you can avoid the temptation to overspend or dip into funds you have set aside for other expenses. Moreover, sticking to a cash-only system may make you more mindful of your spending habits and less likely to make impulsive purchases.

While the envelope system does require some effort, it is a useful tool for anyone looking to take control of their finances. Plus, with digital apps and spreadsheets, you can apply the envelope budget to your digital life. Overall, the envelope budget can be a rewarding way to cultivate a more mindful and strategic approach to your finances.

50/30/20 Budget

The 50/30/20 budgeting rule is a tool that individuals can use to manage their money effectively and save for the future without feeling overwhelmed or deprived. The simplicity of this rule lies in its ability to balance the "must-haves" with the "wants" while still enabling individuals to save a significant portion of their income. By allocating 50% of after-tax income to needs, such as rent, groceries, and utility bills, individuals can comfortably maintain their standard of living without creating financial stress. The next 30% can go towards affording those extras we all crave, like dining out, traveling, or buying the latest phone. The last 20% should go directly towards savings for emergencies, investments, and debt repayment.

This method of budgeting has pros and cons. One of the primary advantages is the simplicity of the approach and its capacity to create serious savings. As a result, many people find it easier to stick with since the breakdown is easy to understand and manage. Additionally, this rule provides an opportunity to save without making significant sacrifices in the present; thus, individuals using this rule can still enjoy life while building towards their goals. However, one of the shortcomings of this rule is that it is not tailored to individual circumstances, and some people may have needs that exceed 50% of their income. For those individuals, finding creative ways to cut costs without compromising their needs could be a challenge. Along those lines, the rule's focus on percentages rather than dollar values can be difficult for people living in costly parts of the country or those without stable incomes.

It remains an effective tool for managing personal finances, as it offers a straightforward and achievable template for reaching financial goals. Implementing automated systems, such as auto-deposits and automatic billing, can help people stick to it. If followed, the rule could prove beneficial to individuals hoping to save money for things they are passionate about or even just toward a rainy day.

> "By managing your finances through budgeting, you can make informed financial decisions, avoid debt and overspending, and work towards a stable and prosperous future."

The "No" Budget Budget

The "No Budget" method may sound too good to be true. Still, it can work wonders for those who find traditional budgeting methods too time-consuming and stressful. With this method, you don't have to meticulously track every single expense or divide your income into different categories. Instead, you simply need to have a clear understanding of your expected expenses and income and be deliberate about moving your money around each month. The biggest advantage of the "No Budget" method is its ease and flexibility - you won't have to spend hours poring over spreadsheets or apps, and you can adjust your financial plan as needed. However, it's not without drawbacks - since you won't have a strict budget to follow, you may be more prone to overspending or neglecting essential expenses. This method may not be the best fit for those who prefer a more structured approach to managing their money. But for those who want a simpler way to stay on top of their finances, the "No Budget" method can be a game changer.

How to do the no-budget budget

- **Pay bills as soon as you get paid:** Prioritize paying all bills as soon as you get paid to ensure they take priority.
- **Next take care of debt and savings:** Determine the amount of money you can afford to save or put towards debt each month based on your income, bills, and expenses. Do this right after you get paid to avoid accidentally spending this money.
- **If you don't have it, don't spend it:** Spend what's left on your variable expenses until you get paid again. Make a rule to only spend what's in your bank account and stop spending when the money is gone.
- **Do not buy on credit:** Avoid using credit cards to prevent overspending since you're working with an approximate budget.
- **What to do with leftover money:** At the end of the pay period/month, plan how to use any extra money by paying off debt, investing, or saving it.
- **Create a cushion:** Keep a buffer of at least $100 in your checking account as a precaution in case you overspend or don't keep track of your account for a while.

- **Keep on top of balances and bills**: Regularly check your bank account at least once a week to make sure you're not overspending or missing any bills or savings goals.
- **Automate as much as possible:** Set up automatic savings and automatic bill payments from your checking account.
- **Review monthly:** Spend 20 minutes at the end of each month reviewing your bank statements and making necessary adjustments for the next month. Take note of any upcoming expenses that aren't part of your everyday spending, such as car maintenance or property taxes.
- **Give yourself a pat on the back:** Celebrate your progress, no matter how small, and keep working towards your financial goals with the No Budget, Budget method.

BUDGETING FOR A BRIGHT FINANCIAL FUTURE

Personal budgeting is an essential financial management tool that helps take control of finances and improve overall financial well-being. People can prioritize their spending, establish savings goals, and make informed financial decisions by tracking income and expenses. Personal budgeting provides a clear picture of an individual's financial situation, which helps reduce stress and increase economic security. Budgeting allows people to prepare for unexpected expenses and emergencies, avoiding debt and overspending. By developing a healthy relationship with money through budgeting, individuals can work towards a stable and prosperous future, achieving their financial goals and creating a better life for themselves and their families.

YOUNG PEOPLE CHANGING THE WORLD

Melati and Isabel Wijen

Melati and Isabel Wijen are two inspiring young activists who have made an incredible impact on the world. At a young age, they recognized the alarming amount of plastic pollution in their native country of Indonesia and set out to make a change. They founded the NGO "Bye Bye Plastic Bags," which began as a campaign to ban plastic bags from Bali but expanded to advocating for the ban of single-use plastics worldwide. Their hard work and dedication did not go unnoticed, as they were able to petition the Indonesian government to ban plastic bags, straws, and styrofoam in 2019. Their efforts have since extended far beyond Indonesia, with teams in over 50 locations around the globe. Melati and Isabel have used their platform to raise awareness about the dangers of plastic pollution by speaking at 450 events and reaching over 100,000 students. Their actions have not only helped in reducing plastic pollution but also served as an inspiration for young people around the world to become active in making a difference in the world.

Try this:

Ask a friend or family member about their budget and what works for them and what doesn't.

Try out one of the mentioned budgets for a month and see how it works for you. What did you like and did not like about it?

A PLACE FOR MY THOUGHTS

- How can I balance my current needs with my long-term financial goal
- When I run into financial challenges, how can I overcome them
- How can I balance my spending with my priorities and goals?

9

CREDIT WHAT?

"There are many things in life that will catch your eye, but only a few will catch your heart. Pursue these."

— MICHAEL NOLAN

As young adults venture out into the world, they encounter situations where credit and loans become an integral part of their financial lives. It is crucial for them to learn about the benefits and drawbacks of managing credit wisely and utilizing loans responsibly. Credit scores, loan interests, and payment deadlines may seem daunting at first, but learning the basics can pave the way for financial freedom and success. This chapter will explore the world of credit and loans, uncovering important information that every young adult should know to make informed decisions about their finances. Whether it's purchasing a car, renting an apartment, or applying for a student loan, learning the ins and outs of credit and loans will help young adults navigate the financial landscape with confidence.

WHAT A CREDIT SCORE IS AND WHY IT MATTERS

A credit score is an essential piece of information that determines your creditworthiness and the likelihood of being approved for loans and credit products. It is a three-digit number that ranges from 300 to 850, with a higher score indicating a more impressive credit history. Your credit score is calculated based on various factors, including your repayment history, total levels of debt, length of credit history, and other factors that showcase your creditworthiness. Lenders use these scores to evaluate and determine your creditworthiness. They can play a significant role in the approval process for mortgages, personal loans, credit cards, and other credit products. Credit scores are not limited to just loan approvals; they can also affect employment opportunities, rental applications, and utility services.

Fair Isaac Corp., now called FICO, developed the credit score model and remains the most commonly used credit scoring system across the United States. Though a high credit score won't guarantee loan approvals or lower interest rates, building and maintaining a good credit score is a reliable way to improve your financial well-being.

WHY IT MATTERS

A good credit score is crucial for obtaining credit, as it plays a significant role in a lender's decision to approve or deny a loan application.

- A higher credit score increases the likelihood of getting approved for loans, credit cards, and mortgages, while lower credit scores may lead to higher interest rates, larger down payments, or outright rejection of the loan application.
- Lenders consider a credit score of 700 or above good.
- Credit scores are also used by landlords, utility companies, and mobile phone companies to determine deposits for services.
- Every creditor has its own criteria for lending and credit score ranges.

HOW IT IS CALCULATED

Your credit score is calculated by evaluating five main factors. The factors include payment history, amounts owed, length of credit history, types of credit, and new credit.

- **Your history:** Your payment history is the most significant factor in calculating your credit score, accounting for 35%. It evaluates whether you have paid your bills on time, how many late payments you have had, and how late they were.
- **The amount:** The amount you owe on credit or credit utilization makes up 30% of your credit score. This factor takes into account the percentage of credit you have used compared to the credit available to you.
- **History length:** The length of your credit history makes up 15% of your credit score. Lenders consider longer credit histories less risky as they show a more detailed payment history.
- **Diversity:** Credit mix, or the variety of credit types you can manage, is 10% of the score and includes installment and revolving credit. Both installment credit, such as car loans or mortgage loans, and revolving credit, such as credit cards, can show lenders that you can manage various types of credit.
- **Too much at once:** Finally, new credit makes up the remaining 10% of your credit score. Lenders view too many recent applications for credit as a potential sign that you may be desperate for credit, which can negatively affect your credit score.

How do you establish credit?

Here are some proven ways to help you establish credit:

- **Open a credit card:** This is the most common way to establish credit. Look for a card with no annual fee, a low-interest rate, and a credit limit that is within your means. Make sure to use it responsibly and pay your bills on time every month.
- **Become an authorized user:** If you can't qualify for a credit card on your own, you can become an authorized user on someone else's account. This will allow you to use the card, but keep in mind that the primary account holder is responsible for payments.
- **Take out a credit-builder loan:** Credit-builder loans are designed to help you build a credit history by borrowing a smaller amount and paying it back over time. These loans are typically offered by credit unions and community banks, and they report payments to the credit bureaus. Creating a savings account to repay the loan with small payments over time is a good idea.
- **Set up a joint account or get a co-signer:** If you need help qualifying for credit on your own, consider setting up a joint account or getting a co-signer. Keep in mind that both parties are

responsible for payments, so make sure you can trust your co-signer.

- **Pay your bills on time:** More and more companies are using alternative scoring methods that consider things like rent payments, phone bills, and bank account transactions to determine creditworthiness. Paying your bills on time can help you establish credit even if you don't have a traditional credit history. This is a great time to use the automatic payment tools from your bank.

Building good credit can take time, so be patient and consistent with your payments. With a little effort, you can establish a solid credit history.

How do you improve your credit score?

- **Make payments on time:** Late or missed payments can significantly impact your credit score. Set reminders for due dates and consider enrolling in automatic payments to ensure your bills are paid on time each month.
- **Keep balances low:** High balances on credit cards can negatively affect your credit score. Try to keep your balance below 30% of your available credit limit.
- **Monitor your credit report:** Check your credit report regularly to ensure accuracy and to catch any potential identity theft. You're entitled to one

free annual credit report from each major credit reporting agency. The big three are Equifax, TransUnion, and Experian.

- **Limit new credit applications:** Applying for too much credit within a short period of time can impact your credit score negatively. Be mindful when applying for new credit and only apply for what you need. This includes retail credit cards offered at the checkout for a percent off of that day's purchase. They are tempting, but remember it will reflect on your credit report and another thing for you to manage.

- **Keep old credit accounts open:** The age of credit accounts is a factor in your credit score, so keeping your older accounts open can be beneficial. Consider using these accounts periodically to keep them active.

- **Be patient:** Improving your credit score takes time, so don't expect overnight results. Stay committed to good credit habits, and your score will gradually improve over time.

Remember, improving your credit score is possible with dedication and a willingness to make positive changes. With these tips, you can take control of your credit and set yourself up for a solid financial future.

WHEN CREDIT SCORES GO BAD

How to Handle Credit Score Issues

- **Keep an eye on it:** Check your credit reports regularly for incorrect information that may negatively affect your credit score. Under the Fair Credit Reporting Act, you have the right to dispute inaccurate information.
- **File a dispute:** If you find incorrect information, file a dispute with the credit reporting agencies. The agencies are required to investigate your dispute and update or remove the information if necessary.
- **Ask for explanation if denied:** If you are denied credit, request an adverse action letter, which will explain why you were denied and allow you to receive a free copy of the credit report that was used in the decision.
- **Be prompt:** Be aware that you only have 60 days to order your free credit report after receiving an adverse action letter, so act quickly.
- **Use the web to reach out:** Each of the three major credit bureaus has a web page with information on ordering negative action credit reports, which can be easier and quicker than sending a letter or making a phone call.

Don't give up hope if you are denied credit or find incorrect information on your credit report. By taking action and following these steps, you can improve your credit score and get back on track.

WHAT HAPPENS IF YOU ARE DENIED A LOAN OR CREDIT

Credit Cards

What you should know before getting one

- **It can make or Break Your Credit:** The most important thing to know before getting a credit card is that it can either build or ruin your credit, so it's crucial to use it responsibly.
- **Make a Deposit:** Many credit cards require a security deposit, making it easier for beginners to get approved.
- **Do your research:** Before applying for a credit card, make sure to research the rates and fees associated with it. You should be able to find this information online or by calling the credit card company.
- **Avoid Fees:** While credit card fees may seem daunting, many of them are avoidable. For example, you can avoid the annual fee by choosing a card that doesn't charge one.

- **Avoid interest:** Interest is entirely preventable if you pay your balance in full each month. If you carry a balance, pay more than the minimum to avoid accumulating interest.
- **Don't be Late:** Paying your credit card bill late can come at a high cost, including late fees and a negative impact on your credit score.
- **Stay within 30%:** It's essential to avoid getting too close to your credit limit, as this can cause your credit score to drop. Ideally, you should use no more than 30% of your available monthly credit.
- **Be Responsible:** By using a credit card responsibly, you can build a positive credit history and qualify for better credit cards and loan rates in the future. Make sure you understand the terms and conditions, keep track of your spending, and pay your bills on time.
- **Everyday Use:** Some credit cards also offer rewards or cash-back programs, so it's worth considering these options if you plan to use your card for everyday purchases.
- **Plan for the future:** Your credit card use today can have a big impact on your financial future. Think about your goals and how your credit card fits into your overall financial plan.
- **Consider your Needs:** Finally, if you're unsure about which credit card to choose, consider reaching out to a financial advisor or doing more

research online to find the best option for your needs and financial situation.

"Rules" regarding credit cards

Here's what you need to know about how they work

• **It is a loan:** With a credit card, you're borrowing money from a lender to make purchases rather than using your own funds from a checking or savings account.

• **Keep track of your max:** Your credit limit is the maximum amount you can borrow at any given time. You can borrow up to that limit, but remember, it is recommended to keep your balance under 30% of your credit limit.

• **Pay at least the minimum:** Every month, you'll receive a statement that outlines your charges and balance. You'll need to make a minimum payment by the due date to avoid late fees and penalties.

• **Interest adds quickly:** If you don't pay your balance in full each month, interest charges will be added to your balance. This can quickly escalate, particularly if you only make minimum payments.

• **Read fine print**: Credit cards come with various terms and conditions, including fees, interest rates, and rewards programs. Be sure to read the fine print before signing up for a credit card.

• **Look for rewards that suit you:** Credit cards can offer benefits such as cash-back rewards, travel perks, and purchase protection.

THINKING ABOUT TAKING OUT A LOAN?

Personal loans and what you should know

How to Get a Personal Loan

- **How much will you need?** Determine how much cash you need, factoring in origination fees (any upfront costs), by using a personal loan calculator. There are many loan calculators online.
- **Find out your credit score:** Check your credit score to see if you meet the minimum requirement of at least fair credit (580-669), with good and excellent credit (above 670) giving you the best chance of approval and a competitive interest rate.
- **What are options that could help you?** Consider your options; these may include a co-signer if necessary or a secured personal loan with collateral, such as a vehicle, house, or cash in a savings account or certificate of deposit, in exchange for more favorable terms.
- **What type do you need?** Determine which type of loan is best for your situation, with some lenders allowing flexible use of funds and others

only approving specific purposes such as small business funding.

- **Shop around for lenders:** Research the best possible interest rates from traditional banks, credit unions, and online lenders, comparing several lenders and loan types to see what you qualify for
- **What rates are available?** Utilize prequalification options some online lenders offer to fully understand the rates available to you without hurting your credit score.
- **Complete the application:** Apply with the lender of your choice, either online or in person at your local bank or credit union.
- **Gather your information:** Be prepared to provide personal information, income and employment information, and the reason for the loan on the application.
- **Double-check details:** Review the complete terms and conditions of the loan, including fees and repayment period, to avoid hidden fees and other pitfalls.
- **Make a repayment plan:** Ensure you have a solid plan for repayment and make payments on time to avoid late fees and harming your credit score.

Different kinds of personal loans

- **Debt consolidation loans:** One of the most popular reasons people take out personal loans is to consolidate existing debts. By doing so, you can reduce the monthly payments you have to make and potentially receive a lower interest rate, helping you get out of debt faster and with less financial stress.
- **Credit card refinancing loans:** If you have credit card debt with high-interest
- **Rates:** A personal loan can be a great way to pay it off and save money in the long run. Many personal loan providers offer lower interest rates than credit card companies, so you can consolidate your balances and pay them off at a more affordable rate.
- **Home improvement loans:** Whether you want to upgrade your kitchen or overhaul your entire home, a personal loan can help you pay for big-ticket home improvement projects. This way, you don't have to put it all on credit cards or take out a home equity loan, which can be risky if you can't make the payments.
- **Medical loans:** Health expenses can quickly add up, which is why some people turn to personal loans to cover medical bills, procedures, and other related expenses. This can be a helpful way to

decrease the immediate financial burden and pay the debt down over time.

- **Emergency loans:** Sometimes things happen unexpectedly, and we need access to cash quickly. Whether it's a car breakdown, an unexpected medical expense, or a leaky roof, an emergency loan can provide the funds you need to cover the costs and get back on track.
- **Wedding loans:** Weddings can be expensive, but with a personal loan, you can spread out the cost of your special day over several years rather than paying for everything all at once. This can be especially helpful if you're on a tight budget but still want to celebrate your love in style.

How to apply

- **Gather documentation:** Gather your latest pay stubs, bank statements, tax forms, and other documentation that lenders may require.
- **Complete the application:** Fill out the application accurately and truthfully. Be prepared to provide personal information such as your name, address, and contact information.
- **Specify loan amount and terms:** Indicate how much money you want to borrow and for how long. Consider factors such as interest rates, fees, and repayment period.

- **Wait for approval:** After submitting your application, wait for the lender to review it and make a decision. This process can take several days.
- **Provide additional documentation:** If the lender requires additional documentation, provide it promptly to speed up the process.
- **Accept loan terms:** If approved, review the loan documents and accept the terms. Be sure to understand all fees, interest rates, and other terms before accepting.
- **Receive loan funds:** Once you accept the loan terms, you can usually receive the loan funds within a week or as soon as one to two business days with some online lenders.
- **Start making payments:** Create a plan to make monthly payments and pay off the loan. Set up automatic payments to avoid missing payments and consider paying extra each month to save on interest.

Interest rates

Interest rates are a fundamental aspect of the modern financial system, representing the cost of borrowing money or the payment received for lending money. While this concept might seem straightforward, the intricacies of how interest rates are determined and applied can be complex. However, understanding these nuances can help individuals make better financial decisions and take advantage of the opportunities presented to them. There are plenty of opportunities to earn interest through banking products such as savings accounts, money market accounts, and CDs. Borrowers can take advantage of fixed or variable interest rates to manage their costs over the course of a loan. Whether you are saving for the future or looking to finance a major purchase, interest rates are a crucial factor to consider, and with careful research and evaluation, you can find options that work best for your unique financial situation.

How it works

When you deposit your money into a savings account or a certificate of deposit (CD), you are essentially lending that money to the bank. In return, the bank pays you interest on your deposit. The interest rate you earn will depend on several factors, including the type of account, the amount you deposit, and prevailing market conditions. Financial institutions will then lend out these funds to others at a higher rate than they are paying you in order to make a profit. A higher interest rate can result in more money in your pocket, while a lower interest rate may mean less money earned over time. With a basic understanding of how interest rates work, you can make informed decisions to shop around and find the best place to save and invest your money.

"A good credit score is crucial for obtaining credit, as it plays a significant role in a lender's decision to approve or deny a loan application."

CAR LOANS AND WHAT YOU SHOULD KNOW

Car loans are a vital tool that can help you achieve your dream when buying a car. However, before jumping into taking out a car loan, it is essential to know what you should look out for and what you can do to secure the best deal.

- **Credit Score:** Different lenders have different criteria, and the minimum score needed to qualify will vary depending on which company is providing the financing.
- **Time Span:** When applying for loans, keep the process within a two-week period to help reduce the negative impact on your credit score. All inquiries made during that time will be considered as one, reducing the hit on your score.
- **Understand dealer financing:** While dealership financing may sound like a good deal, comparing their terms to what your bank or credit union offers is important. Remember that the special offers may only be available to the most highly qualified buyers.
- **Get Pre-approved:** If you decide to go with a bank loan, a pre-approved offer guarantees that

you have the financing to cover the cost of the car you want and lets you focus on the vehicle choice without having to worry if you can swing the monthly payment.

- **Calculate Total Costs:** It's essential to understand the factors that go into setting your monthly car payment, including additional costs such as taxes, fees, and extra features. Always negotiate whether or not the vehicle includes some extras. Before agreeing upon the price, know when to say no if the cost isn't within your budget.
- **Borrow within Your Budget:** Consider borrowing an amount that allows your budget the flexibility to pay more than the monthly payment amount to help improve your credit score for the next auto loan after this one.

HOME LOANS AND WHAT YOU SHOULD KNOW

What to do before you apply

Understand where you are financially: Before applying for a home loan, it is vital to understand and take steps to improve your financial standing. Your credit score is a key factor in determining your eligibility for a mortgage loan and the interest rate you will receive. Checking your credit score and ensuring any errors are corrected, and debts are paid off can greatly improve your chances of being approved for a loan and receiving a lower interest rate.

- **Debt-to-income ratio (DTI):** Lenders will also examine your debt-to-income ratio, which measures how much of your income is used to pay off recurring debts such as student and car loans. It is recommended that your DTI equal no more than 43% of your gross monthly income to ensure you can comfortably make your mortgage payments.

- **Save for costs:** Saving for a down payment and closing costs is also crucial before applying for a home loan. A larger down payment can result in a lower interest rate and monthly mortgage payment. While a 20% down payment is not required, a down payment of less than 20% will result in the added expense of private mortgage insurance (PMI).

- **Budget to determine what you can afford**: Creating a house budget using a home affordability calculator can help determine the maximum home price you can afford based on your income, credit score, monthly debt, down payment, and location. This can prevent you from overextending your finances and being unable to make mortgage payments.

- **Learn your options:** Researching loan options and comparing lenders can help you find the best home loan for your financial situation. Consider the loan options available, interest rates, fees, and the reputation and customer satisfaction of potential lenders.

- **Get Pre-approved:** Obtaining preapproval from a lender before applying for a mortgage loan is recommended. This requires submitting identification, bank statements, and tax returns to determine your creditworthiness and the amount of money you can borrow.

Taking these steps before applying for a home loan can greatly improve your chances of being approved and receiving a favorable interest rate, leading to many years of financial benefit.

Types of loans

Conventional Loan

Homebuyers often prefer conventional loans due to their flexibility and range of options. Unlike government-backed loans, they are not restricted by size limits and can be used to purchase a range of home types, including second or vacation homes. Conventional loans offer borrowers greater control over paying mortgage insurance, which can save them money over the life of the loan. Unlike some government loans, conventional loans typically don't charge program fees, making them a more affordable option for many homebuyers. Conventional loans offer borrowers a wide range of choices in loan structure, enabling them to tailor their loans to their unique financial situation and borrowing goals.

VA Loans

VA home loans are an excellent option for eligible veterans, active-duty service members, and surviving spouses looking to become homeowners. These loans, backed by the Department of Veterans Affairs, offer a range of benefits, such as waived down payments and lower interest rates, making it easier for borrowers to purchase their homes. Not only do VA loans provide affordable financing for eligible homebuyers, but they also have flexible eligibility requirements, including no minimum credit score required. There is also no private mortgage insurance (PMI) requirement, which can lead to lower monthly payments for borrowers.

FHA Loans

FHA loans are an excellent option for those with lower credit scores and need to buy a home. These loans are backed by the Federal Housing Administration, which means that the risk is taken on by the government, not the lender. As a result, many lenders are more willing to approve those with imperfect credit scores, which is a huge benefit to those who don't have substantial savings for a down payment or don't meet the stricter lender requirements for conventional loans. The down payment for FHA loans can be as low as 3.5%, which is one of the main benefits of these types of loans. However, it is important to note that FHA loans have additional costs to offset the lower credit score requirements, such as an upfront and annual mortgage insurance premium (MIP).

USDA Loans

USDA loans for homes are government-backed mortgages designed to empower individuals in low to moderate-income rural communities to achieve homeownership. These loans offer a bunch of benefits that are often not available with traditional mortgages. One of the most attractive features is that borrowers can purchase a property without giving a down payment, which can be a significant financial burden for those looking to get on the housing ladder. It further helps loan approval for lower-income families and individuals, as no private mortgage insurance is required. These loans may offer competitive interest rates, saving borrowers money over time. The USDA loan program also encourages early payments, as there are typically no prepayment penalties. There is, however, a required guarantee fee that the borrower must pay, which serves as an insurance fee for the lender.

What NOT to do before you apply for a loan

• **No large purchases:** Do not make large purchases on credit or apply for new credit accounts before applying for a mortgage. This could negatively affect your credit score and your ability to qualify for a mortgage.

• **Get a different job:** Do not change or quit your current job before applying for a mortgage. Lenders prefer borrowers who have a stable employment history and income.

• **No Co-signing:** Do not co-sign on any loans for friends or family before applying for a mortgage. This could increase your debt-to-income ratio and make it harder for you to get approved for a mortgage.

• **Take money out of your retirement account:** Avoid borrowing money from your retirement account, as this can also increase your debt-to-income ratio and impact your ability to qualify for a mortgage.

• **No big change in your accounts:** Do not make large deposits or withdrawals from your bank account without keeping a detailed transaction record. Unexplained transactions could lead to suspicion.

• **Do not default:** Avoid defaulting on existing loans or credit accounts, as this can severely damage your credit score and lower your chances of qualifying for a mortgage.

• **Do not fudge the facts:** Do not misrepresent any information on your mortgage application, such as your income or employment history. This could lead to fraud charges and serious legal consequences.

• **No late payments:** Do not make any late payments on your existing loans or credit accounts, as this could negatively impact your credit score and your ability to qualify for a mortgage.

• **Have many loans at once:** Avoid applying for multiple mortgages or loans within a short period of time, as this can suggest to lenders that you are desperate for financing and increase their risk of lending to you.

How long does it all take?

Obtaining a mortgage is a process that requires a bit of patience. Once you decide to apply for a mortgage, the initial step is to get pre-approved. The preapproval process typically takes one to two days, during which the lender analyzes and verifies your income, assets, and credit score. After the preapproval, you can start your home search, which can take anywhere from a few weeks to several months, depending on the housing market and your preferences. Once you find the right property and make an offer, the lender usually takes around 30-45 days to finalize the loan. During this period, you'll have to provide additional documentation, such as bank statements and tax returns, which may delay the process if not provided promptly. Ultimately, the time it takes to get a mortgage depends on multiple factors, including your financial situation, creditworthiness, and the complexity of the loan.

Unlocking the Power of Credit and Loans.

Knowledge of credit scores, loan interest rates, and payment deadlines may seem intimidating at first, but taking the time to learn the basics will pave the way for a lifetime of responsible financial decision-making. Exploring the world of credit and loans has revealed the benefits and drawbacks of managing credit wisely and using loans responsibly. Whether it's buying a car, financing a dream vacation, or applying for a student loan, knowing how to navigate the financial landscape with confidence will lead to a brighter financial future.

YOUNG PEOPLE CHANGING THE WORLD

Bao Nakashima

Bao Nakashima is an exceptional young writer from Japan who has achieved remarkable success at an incredibly young age. His journey began with being mercilessly bullied at school, which prompted him to cease attending classes. Nakashima's drive and determination led him to craft his own curriculum, in which he focused on particular authors and subjects. He poured his heart and soul into his notebooks, and it was through these writings that he caught the attention of an editor, who was impressed by the maturity of his thoughts. These efforts culminated in the publication of his book *Seeing, Knowing, Thinking*, a best-seller in Japan that has since been translated into multiple languages. In addition to his impressive literary achievements, Nakashima was selected to participate in the distinguished ROCKET Project, a program for gifted children supported by the Nippon Foundation and the University of Tokyo, which further attests to his exceptional intellect and talent. Despite his hardships, Bao has proven himself to be an exemplar of tenacity, creativity, and perseverance and undoubtedly has a bright future ahead of him.

Try this:

Get your credit score report. Was it worse or better than you thought it would be?

Do some research about what improves your credit score and what decreases it.

Pick an item you would like to have (your dream car, for instance), and figure out the delivered price you would pay and the amount of loan payment.

How many months/years is the loan for?

Would you be able to pay it for that length of time?

What would the numbers be for a more economical car, and what is the difference?

A PLACE FOR MY THOUGHTS

- What does financial freedom look like for me?

- How can I use my credit and loans to get what I need to be successful and happy?
- Would buying your dream car be worth it even if it was financially tight for you to pay for the length of the loan?

INVEST EARLY!

"The best revenge is massive success."

— FRANK SINATRA

T oday's world is constantly evolving and changing, and the need to take control of our financial future has become more critical than ever before. Young adults often find themselves waiting for the "perfect" moment to invest, thinking they don't have enough knowledge or money to start. However, waiting for the "perfect" moment, for when the obstacles are out of the way, might lead us to miss out on the potential benefits of starting early. Starting to invest early on in our lives can have profound implications on our financial future, including the ability to build wealth, afford a comfortable retirement, and achieve financial freedom. This chapter will explore the importance of investing early in life, the benefits and potential risks associated with it, and offer practical advice on how to get started.

WHY IT'S WISE TO INVEST EARLY

Investing is an important part of growing your wealth, and it's never too early to start. Various investment options are available, each with its own advantages and risks. It's important to have a diverse portfolio, which means investing in more than one type of asset.

- **Discipline:** Investment at an early age teaches the importance of financial independence and discipline.
- **Recover is easier:** Starting early allows for more recovery time in case of investment losses.
- **Good Habit to Start:** Early investments develop a habit of saving more.
- **Take more risks:** Young investors have more risk-taking ability than older ones, leading to more opportunities for higher returns.
- **Increase time value:** Early investments lead to compounding returns and increase the time value of money.
- **Security:** Early investments lead to a more secure future, providing a safety net during tough times.
- **Lose Debt quicker:** Investing early allows for the opportunity to become a creditor instead of a debtor.

- **Support for your long-term plan:** Early-age investments increase the probability of reaching financial stability at a young age, supporting retirement plans.
- **Tech makes it easy:** Technology and online platforms make researching and investing in higher returns more accessible than ever.
- **You can do it in small increments:** Even in smaller amounts, investing early provides more time for money to mature and build wealth.

What you should invest in as a teen/young adult

- **High-Yield Savings Accounts:** A HYSA is a great way for young adults to earn a return on their money without taking on any risk. It provides a higher interest rate than a standard savings account and is a good option for those looking for liquidity and low-risk investments.
- **Certificates of Deposit:** CDs require individuals to lock their money away for a specific period of time, but in return, they offer higher interest rates than savings accounts. It is a risk-free investment option that guarantees a return on investment at the end of the term.
- **Stocks:** Stocks provide the opportunity to own a share in a company and earn money through capital gains and dividends. It's essential to conduct thorough research and analysis before

investing in individual stocks, as they can be volatile and risky.

- **Bonds:** Bonds are a type of debt security that provides a predictable income stream. It is a good option for those who prefer a stable, low-risk investment option.

- **Funds:** Mutual funds and ETFs are pooled investment options that provide exposure to many different securities in a single investment. They offer diversification and are an excellent option for young adults who are just starting and have limited funds to invest.

Opening an Investment Account for Teens

Opening an investment account for young adults can provide them with a solid financial foundation as they embark on their journey toward financial independence. To open an investment account for a young adult, it is important to first determine their financial goals, risk tolerance, and investment horizon. Once these details are established, a custodial account can be opened to allow an adult to invest on behalf of the minor until they reach legal adulthood. UGMA and UTMA accounts are the most common types of custodial accounts. They can hold financial assets like stocks, bonds, mutual funds, and cash, with UTMA accounts also capable of holding physical assets like real estate. Additionally, custodial individual retirement accounts allow teens to start saving for retirement before they reach adulthood. It is important to note that assets in a custodial account legally belong to the child, which means that any money put into the account is considered an irrevocable gift and cannot be taken back. Investing in a custodial account for a young adult can set them on the path toward financial independence.

How old do you have to be to invest in stocks?

The question of age limit frequently arises when it comes to investing in the stock market. According to the law, investors under the age of 18 cannot establish their brokerage accounts and manage their investment portfolios. Nonetheless, investing can start at any age as long as an adult opens a brokerage account on behalf of a child, even a newborn. However, the adult custodian has complete control of the account, including all investment decisions, until the child reaches the age of 18. This means that an adult must supervise and make the final call on all investment decisions until the minor can act on their own.

Who pays taxes on custodial accounts?

Custodial accounts are subject to federal tax rules that govern children's unearned income, colloquially dubbed as the "kiddie tax." Under this tax regime, the assets in custodial accounts belong to the child, and the taxation depends on the amount of unearned income they receive. The kiddie tax allows the first $1,150 of unearned income to be exempt from federal taxes in 2023. The following

$1,150 is taxed at the child's tax rate. However, suppose the child earns more than $2,300. In that case, the excess amount is taxed at the parent's tax rate to eliminate wealthy parents' loop of transferring assets to their children to avoid higher taxes. Keep in mind the kiddie tax does not apply to earned income from a job or self-employment, so the child is responsible for paying taxes in these cases. Parents may consider setting up a Roth IRA or saving for college through a 529 investment account to avoid kiddie tax. Understanding the taxation rules on custodial accounts is crucial for parents to manage their children's finances effectively.

Yes, You Should be Thinking About Retirement and Why

Starting to plan for retirement as a young adult may seem like an unnecessary inconvenience, especially when there are more pressing financial concerns, such as student loans, car payments, or housing expenses. However, the earlier you start saving for retirement, the more time your money has to grow and compound. This will give them a significant boost to their retirement income. For example, as of 2023, a 25-year-old who saves $5,000 a year at a 6% rate of return will have almost $1 million by the time they turn 65. On the other hand, if they wait until they are 35 to start saving, they will need to contribute over $11,500 a year to reach the same amount by the age of 65. Contributing early to a Roth account is a smart move if you expect your income to increase to a higher tax bracket over your career, as pre-paying taxes now while in a low tax bracket will result in a locked-in, lower tax rate.

"Starting to invest early on in our lives can have profound implications on our financial future, including the ability to build wealth, afford a comfortable retirement, and achieve financial freedom."

401k (what it is and why it matters)

A 401(k) plan is a retirement savings account that is sponsored by an employer and allows employees to contribute a portion of their income toward their retirement fund. These contributions can be pre-tax or post-tax, depending on the type of 401(k) plan offered. If an employee chooses a traditional 401(k) plan, their contributions will come from their pre-tax income, and the withdrawals from the account during retirement will be taxed. On the other hand, with a Roth 401(k) plan, contributions are made with after-tax income, but the withdrawals from the account are tax-free. Some Employers may also contribute to their employees' 401(k) plans, which can help employees save even more for retirement.

Employees are responsible for selecting their specific investments within their accounts from a selection chosen by their employer, which typically includes various mutual funds, target-date funds, and sometimes the employer's own stock. Keep in mind that there are contribution limits in place, which are set by the Internal

Revenue Service and are adjusted periodically for inflation.

What is so great about a 401k plan

In addition to the tax advantages mentioned above, there are other benefits to having a 401(k) account. It offers an easy, automatic way to save for retirement. Since contributions are deducted from your paycheck before you even see the money, you're less likely to spend it and more likely to save it. This can be especially helpful for people who struggle with saving money on their own.

The matching contribution that many employers offer is essentially "free" money. For example, an employer might match 50% of your contributions up to a certain percentage of your salary. This is an excellent perk and can really help boost your retirement savings, as you're essentially doubling your money.

401(k)s offer a variety of investment options. Most plans will offer a mix of stocks, bonds, and other assets that you can choose from. This allows you to tailor your investments to your individual risk tolerance and investment goals. Plus, many plans offer low-cost index funds as an option.

Individuals who have contributed to a Roth IRA can withdraw their initial contributions without incurring any penalty tax as long as they have not reached the age of 59 1/2, thereby granting them flexibility and access to their funds in emergency situations. This differs from the potential penalties associated with early withdrawals from traditional IRAs or 401(k) plans. It is important to note that any earnings accrued within the account cannot be withdrawn before the age of 59 1/2 years without facing potential penalties.

Traditional IRAs

- **Pre-tax:** A traditional IRA is a type of individual retirement account that allows pre-tax contributions.
- **Tax break for that year:** Contributions to a traditional IRA can result in a tax break for that year as the taxable income lowers.
- **Withdrawals are subject to tax:** Withdrawals made during retirement from a traditional IRA will be subject to regular income tax.
- **Open to anyone working:** The eligibility to open a traditional IRA is available to anyone who earns income and wants to plan for retirement.
- **Bank or brokerage:** Traditional IRAs can be opened at a brokerage or bank.
- **Consider different options:** IRAs from a brokerage can allow investment in stocks and bonds, while banks typically offer Certificates of Deposit and savings accounts.

- **Higher returns:** Stocks and bonds can be a sensible choice for long-term goals like retirement due to their higher historical returns.
- **Limits on contributions:** There are annual contribution limits for traditional IRAs. In 2023, the contribution limit is $6,500 for individuals under 50.
- **Limited on the source of contributions:** Traditional IRA contributions require earned income. For instance, you cannot add money that you were given. Money from other retirement accounts can also be rolled over to add to the IRA.

How to open a Traditional IRA

There are two broad approaches you can take: hands-on or hands-off investing.

- Hands-on approach- you'll have greater control over your investments. Still, you'll also need to do more research and be comfortable deciding what to buy and sell. One option is to open an account with an online broker, giving you access to a wide range of securities, including stocks, bonds, and mutual funds. Each provider will have its fees and minimum requirements, so it's worth shopping around to find one that suits your needs. You may also want to consider the quality of the broker's research and educational resources, as well as the user-friendliness of their trading platform. Hands-on investing comes with the responsibility of staying informed and making smart investment decisions.

- Hands-off Approach- For those who prefer a hands-off approach, opening a traditional IRA with a robo-advisor may be a good choice. Robo-advisors use algorithms to create and manage portfolios based on your goals, risk tolerance, and time horizon. The benefit of this automated approach is that you don't need to have extensive knowledge of the financial markets or spend time monitoring your investments. Robo-advisors also typically charge lower fees than traditional investment managers, making them an attractive option for those looking to reduce costs. It's important to research and find a provider with a good track record that meets your specific needs. Some factors to consider when choosing a robo-advisor include their investment philosophy, asset allocation strategy, and the level of support they offer.

Roth IRA

A Roth IRA allows individuals to invest their money with after-tax dollars. This means that contributions made to a Roth IRA have already been subjected to income taxes before the money is invested, which differs from a traditional IRA. A Roth IRA's significant advantage is its tax-free income when the individual retires. Not only does this account offer tax-free income, but the money invested in a Roth IRA also grows tax-free. Therefore, the account holder does not pay capital gains taxes on the funds generated over time. These tax-free benefits make a Roth IRA an excellent investment.

Choosing between a Roth IRA and a traditional IRA can be challenging. It is essential to think about when one might pay more taxes. If an individual is currently paying a high tax rate, contributing to a traditional IRA may be beneficial because they can take advantage of tax deductions now. Conversely, if they expect their annual taxes to increase, contributing to a Roth IRA may be more beneficial. An important fact to consider when deciding between the two is that there are income limits on a Roth IRA. Suppose an individual earns above a certain amount in a year. In that case, they may not be eligible to contribute to a Roth IRA.

A Roth IRA can be funded through various means, such as regular contributions, contributions from a spouse, transfers, and IRA rollovers and conversions. There are contribution limits on a Roth IRA.

SEP IRA

- **Individual:** A Simplified Employee Pension (SEP) is an individual retirement account (IRA) that an employer or self-employed individual can establish.
- **Lower costs:** It is an attractive option for business owners due to lower start-up and operating costs compared to traditional employer-sponsored retirement plans.
- **Higher level than IRA:** SEP IRAs allow employers to contribute to their retirement at higher levels than a traditional IRA allows.
- **You can skip lower income years:** SEP IRAs allow employers to skip contributions during years when business is down.
- **Much the same as an IRA:** Contributions to SEP IRAs are treated like traditional IRAs for tax purposes. They also allow the same investment options and the same transfer and rollover rules.
- **Tax deduction:** The employer receives a tax deduction for the amount contributed to SEP IRA accounts.
- **Employee makes investment decisions:** The employer does not make the investment decisions. The IRA trustee (it could be a bank or a credit union, etc.) determines eligible investments, and the employee makes specific investment decisions.

- **Vested immediately:** Contributions to SEP IRAs are immediately 100% vested.
- **Must first have traditional IRA:** Eligible employees who participate in their employer's SEP plan must establish a traditional IRA to which the employer will deposit SEP contributions.
- **Limited contributions:** Contributions made by employers cannot exceed the lesser of 25% of an employee's compensation or $66,000 in 2023. They are also limited to 25% of wages (or profits) minus the SEP contribution for sole proprietorship businesses.
- **Many of the same rules as IRAs:** Once deposited, SEP contributions become traditional IRA assets and are subject to many traditional IRA rules, including distribution, investment, contribution, and documentation requirements.

YOUNG PEOPLE CHANGING THE WORLD

Yasha Asley

Yasha Asley is a young prodigy who has achieved remarkable things in the field of mathematics. With Iranian heritage and a father who excels at home teaching, Asley completed his A-level exams at the tender age of eight, making him the youngest person ever to do so. He divided his time between primary school and the University of Leicester, where he eventually became a mathematics tutor at the ripe old age of 13. In 2017, Asley earned the distinction of being the "world's youngest professor" after being hired by the University of Leicester to teach mathematics while completing his doctorate. Though there were some concerns about child labor laws, Asley proved to be an exceptional lecturer with a bright future as both a mathematician and a teacher.

Try this:

Save a few dollars and invest in some stocks.

Research what would be a good investment.

What is more important to you when investing in stocks, the beliefs, integrity or mission statement of the company?

A PLACE FOR MY THOUGHTS

- Am I able to "let go" of some money now, even though I won't see the rewards till much later in life?
- How can I align my spending with my values and priorities?
- How can I increase my income and explore new opportunities?

HELP MAKE THE ROAD TO ADULTHOOD EASIER!

"When you learn, teach. When you get, give."
- Maya Angelou

You're firmly on the path toward a bright future... and you can help make that road a little easier for other teenagers like you.

Simply by leaving your honest opinion of this book on Amazon, you'll show new readers where they can find this essential information – and help them discover what they don't know.

LET'S HEAR WHAT YOU THINK!

Thank you for your help. Together, we can make the transition into adulthood less scary for more people.

Did you get value from Life Skills for Teens and Young Adults: Money & Career Edition? Check out the first in the series, Life Skills for Teens and Young Adults: Health edition here:

Scan the QR code below to leave your review on Amazon.

CHARTING YOUR COURSE TO SUCCESS

The transition from high school to a successful career or higher education requires careful planning and decision-making. With the increasing demand for skilled workers in various industries, it is more important than ever for young adults to explore different educational paths and career fields. This book provides readers with a comprehensive guide to navigate this critical time in their lives and offers valuable insights and tools to make informed decisions. From understanding the financial aspects of education to exploring the latest career trends, readers are equipped with the knowledge and skills necessary to achieve their goals and live fulfilling lives. With the right resources and support, young adults can confidently pave the way to a bright and successful future.

A NOTE FROM ANNA B JOELS.

As the author and creator behind this book, I want to extend my deepest gratitude to you for taking the time to read through it. I hope that you were able to glean valuable insights and knowledge that will help to enrich your life experience. It is my sincere desire that these pages serve as a guiding light, providing you with the tools and inspiration that you need to thrive in all areas of your life.

If you found value in this book, I would be deeply grateful if you would consider leaving a review for it and telling others who might benefit about it. Our world needs the kind of positive energy and perspective this book provides, and your help spreading the message would be immensely appreciated.

I welcome any ideas, feedback, or suggestions for this or future books. I believe in the power of collaboration and community, and I am always looking for ways to better serve and support my readers. So please don't hesitate to reach out to me at **thegoodjujujournal@yahoo.com.**

I would be thrilled to hear from you.

As you move forward on your journey, I wish you all the best of luck and remind you that you are important and worthy of all you desire. You have everything within you that you need to succeed, and I truly believe that you will go far in this adventure we call life.

It has been an honor to share my books with you.

Don't forget your bonus chapter
Discover even more practical tools and strategies for navigating life's challenges.

Click the link Below:
https://bit.ly/BonuschapLSFT-MC

Or scan the code below

RESOURCES

Shutterfly. (2019, March 18). *Graduation Quotes and Sayings*. Ideas and Inspiration for Every Occasion | Shutterfly; Shutterfly. https://www.shutterfly.com/ideas/graduation-quotes-and-sayings/

LeBoeuf, R. (2022, June 24). *50 Best Personal Growth Quotes*. Www.snhu.edu. https://www.snhu.edu/about-us/newsroom/education/personal-growth-quotes

Simmons, L. (2021, November 10). *The Pros and Cons of Trade School*. BestColleges.com. https://www.bestcolleges.com/resources/career-training/pros-and-cons-trade-school/

Scholarships.com. (2019). *The Pros And Cons Of Community Colleges - Scholarships.com*. Scholarships.com. https://www.scholarships.com/resources/college-prep/choosing-the-right-school/the-pros-and-cons-of-community-colleges/

Jeremy Anderberg. (2014, March 24). *Is College for Everyone? Part II: The Pros and Cons of Attending a 4-Year College*. The Art of Manliness. https://www.artofmanliness.com/career-wealth/career/is-college-for-everyone-part-ii-the-pros-and-cons-of-attending-a-4-year-college/

Federal Student Aid. (2019, July 5). *Types of Financial Aid*. Federal Student Aid. https://studentaid.gov/understand-aid/types

29 States Now Offer Some Form of Tuition-Free Education, So Why Aren't People Going to College? (2022, June 2). GOBankingRates. https://www.gobankingrates.com/saving-money/education/twenty-nine-states-offer-tuition-free-education-why-people-not-going-college/

Farran Powell, & Kerr, E. (2020). *How to Find and Secure Scholarships for College*. US News & World Report; U.S. News & World Report. https://www.usnews.com/education/best-colleges/paying-for-college/articles/how-to-find-and-secure-scholarships-for-college

Luthi, B. (n.d.). *9 Best Scholarship Search Engines*. Bankrate. https://www.bankrate.com/loans/student-loans/scholarship-search-engines/

(n.d.). https://www.glassdoor.com/blog/guide/what-to-do-at-a-job-fair/

Schubak, A. (2018, March 14). *Read the Stories of 40 Incredible Kids Who Have Changed the World*. Good Housekeeping; Good Housekeeping. https://www.goodhousekeeping.com/life/inspirational-stories/g5188/kids-who-changed-the-world/

Fox, M. (n.d.). *3 Teens Who Are Changing The World*. Forbes. Retrieved October 10, 2023, from https://www.forbes.com/sites/meimeifox/2021/09/08/3-teens-who-are-changing-the-world/?sh=31fa1a132190

Laura. (2023, July 5). *75 Powerful Journal Prompts for Money Mindset and Abundance*. Lauraconteuse.com. https://lauraconteuse.com/journal-prompts-for-money-mindset/

Preparing for University: How UCIL's Courses Improve Critical Thinking and Self-Learning Skills - SYP STUDIOS. https://sypstudios.com/preparing-for-university-how-ucils-courses-improve-critical-thinking-and-self-learning-skills

Online Military Degree Programs: A Comprehensive Guide - Military Media. https://www.militarymedia.net/2023/02/online-military-degree-programs.html

Louisa May Alcott Quotes. http://www.famousquotesandauthors.com/authors/louisa_may_alcott_quotes.html

50 One-Sentence Tips to Help Improve Yourself | Change Your Mind Change Your Life. https://medium.com/change-your-mind/50-one-sentence-tips-to-help-improve-yourself-b9155e3f30e3?source=user_profile---------5---------------------------

Vehicular Homelessness Soars with Housing Prices - Connect CRE. https://www.connectcre.com/stories/vehicular-homelessness-soars-with-housing-prices/

Teenagers Who Changed the World in 2020 | Britannica. https://www.britannica.com/story/teenagers-who-changed-the-world-in-2020

Andreas. (2020, August 20). *32 Key Pros & Cons Of Joining The Army*. E&C. https://environmental-conscience.com/joining-the-army-pros-cons/

Eligibility and Requirements. (n.d.). Goarmy.com. https://www.goarmy.com/how-to-join/requirements.html

Grover, S. (n.d.). *Pros and Cons of the Marines | Synonym*. Classroom.synonym.com. https://classroom.synonym.com/pros-and-cons-of-the-marines-13583789.html

Explorer, C. (2021, October 18). *Pros and Cons of Joining the Military - CampusExplorer*. Www.campusexplorer.com. https://www.campusexplorer.com/student-resources/pros-and-cons-of-joining-the-army/

New York Military Acceptance Rate Us | How to Apply. https://taleheart.com.ng/new-york-military-acceptance-rate-us-how-to-apply/

HOME | ASVAB. https://www.officialasvab.com/

Pellissier, H. (2017, August 25). *42 up-and-coming careers that don't require a 4-year college degree (and 10 to avoid)*. Parenting; GreatSchools. https://www.greatschools.org/gk/articles/great-careers-without-college-degree/

Ways to Embark on a Successful Career Without College. (2019, November 14). FlexJobs Job Search Tips and Blog. https://www.flexjobs.com/blog/post/successful-career-without-college-v2/

College Isn't for Everyone. These Jobs May Be Good Options. (2019). US News & World Report. https://money.usnews.com/money/careers/slideshow/25-best-jobs-that-dont-require-a-college-degree

Skyler, H. (2013). *Six Advantages of Working After High School*. Chron.com. https://work.chron.com/six-advantages-working-after-high-school-15907.html

How do you become a hair stylist? (article). (n.d.). Khan Academy. https://www.khanacademy.org/college-careers-more/career-content/career-profiles-start-a-business/career-profile-hairstylist/a/how-do-you-become-a-hair-stylist

Apprenticeship | U.S. Department of Labor. (n.d.). Www.dol.gov. https://www.dol.gov/general/topic/training/apprenticeship

ISLAMI, Dara Ayu Ning Cahya, and Tarmizi ACHMAD. "ANALISIS PENGARUH REPUTASI ORGANISASI DAN KINERJA KEUANGAN TERHADAP KONTRIBUSI ORGANISASI NIRLABA (Studi Empiris Pada Organisasi Nirlaba Di Indonesia Tahun 2010 - 2014)." 2017, https://core.ac.uk/download/84727998.pdf.

Finding a Job | Indeed.com UK. (n.d.). Indeed Career Guide. https://uk.indeed.com/career-advice/finding-a-job

Indeed Editorial Team. (2023, April 7). *13 Things To Consider When*

Looking for a Job. Indeed Career Guide. https://www.indeed.com/career-advice/finding-a-job/what-to-look-for-in-a-job

becker, joshua. (2010, May 21). *12 Factors to Look For in a Job Other than a Paycheck*. Becoming Minimalist. https://www.becomingminimalist.com/12-factors-to-look-for-in-a-job-other-than-a-paycheck/

MyPerfectResume Staff Writer. (2013, August 18). *How to Use The Internet in Your Job Search*. My Perfect Resume; Myperfect Resume. https://www.myperfectresume.com/career-center/jobs/search/conducting-an-online-job-search

White, M. G., M.A., SHRM-SCP, White, S. M. G., M.A., SHRM-SCP, instructor, S. A. a college, Nonfiction, C. E. with E., Experience, E. W., tips, M. shares, & Policy, advice related to a wide variety of topics R. M. L. about our E. (n.d.). *Tips for Using Job Search Engines*. LoveTo-Know. Retrieved October 10, 2023, from https://jobs.lovetoknow.com/Job_Search_Engines

Contacting Employers of Interest. (2023, April 26). Drexel.edu. https://drexel.edu/scdc/professional-pointers/job-search/contact-employers/

Greenawald, E. (2015, February 4). *45 Things to Do on Social Media to Find Jobs*. Themuse.com; The Muse. https://www.themuse.com/advice/45-things-to-do-on-social-media-to-find-jobs

Individual Instruction. (2013, November 12). The Etiquette School. https://etiquette-school.com/programs/individual-instruction/

Letter of Intent (LOI) How-To Guide + Expert Examples. (2023, February 24). My Perfect Resume. https://www.myperfectresume.com/career-center/jobs/search/letter-of-intent

Zhang, L. (2017, June 30). *The Ultimate Guide to Researching a Company Pre-Interview*. Themuse.com; The Muse. https://www.themuse.com/advice/the-ultimate-guide-to-researching-a-company-preinterview

Thottam, I. (2018, October 29). *15 Interview Questions You Should Be Prepared to Answer This Month*. Glassdoor Blog. https://www.glassdoor.com/blog/interview-questions-you-should-be-prepared-to-answer-this-month/

9 Ways To Sell Yourself In An Interview (+ Examples). (2023, August 7). https://resources.biginterview.com/interviews-101/how-to-sell-yourself-in-an-interview/#:~:text=What%20do%20you%20want%20your

Why You Should Clarify Your Selling Points during Your Interview. (2019, October 24). TRC Staffing Services. https://trcstaffing.com/why-you-should-clarify-your-selling-points-during-your-interview/

MBE, C. D. (2017, February 2). *Four doubts your interviewer has about you – and how to address them.* Viewpoint - Careers Advice Blog. https://social.hays.com/2017/02/02/four-doubts-interviewer-has-about-you-how-address-them/

Green, A. (2020, January 14). *10 Impressive Questions to Ask in a Job Interview.* The Cut. https://www.thecut.com/article/questions-to-ask-in-a-job-interview.html

17 GREAT QUESTIONS to ask in a JOB INTERVIEW! (n.d.). Www.youtube.com. Retrieved October 10, 2023, from https://www.youtube.com/watch?v=8HU2VKH8HJc

Avoid Asking Your Interviewer These Questions. (n.d.). Indeed Career Guide. https://www.indeed.com/career-advice/interviewing/questions-not-to-ask-an-interviewer

TOP 25 LIFE AFTER HIGH SCHOOL QUOTES. (n.d.). A-Z Quotes. Retrieved October 10, 2023, from https://www.azquotes.com/quotes/topics/life-after-high-school.html

Torres, B. (2014, April). *50 Inspirational Career Quotes.* Themuse.com; The Muse. https://www.themuse.com/advice/50-inspirational-career-quotes

8 Young People Who Changed History and the World. (2020, January 24). The Shutterstock Blog. https://www.shutterstock.com/blog/young-people-who-changed-history

Team Culture: Identifiers, Benefits, and How to Build One that Works | Glassdoor. (n.d.). Glassdoor Blog. https://www.glassdoor.com/blog/guide/team-culture/

25+ Pay It Forward Quotes To Remind You To Be Kind | Kidadl. (n.d.). Kidadl.com. Retrieved November 8, 2023, from https://kidadl.com/quotes/pay-it-forward-quotes-to-remind-you-to-be-kind

Cooks-Campbell, A. (2021, May 13). *How to have a good work-life balance (hint: It's not just about time).* Betterup. https://www.betterup.com/blog/how-to-have-good-work-life-balance

How to "Unplug" From Work: Tips for a Healthy Work/Life Balance. (2020,

June 18). Wanderlust Movement | a South Africa Travel Blog. https://www.wanderlustmovement.org/how-to-unplug-from-work/

Why Are Vacations Important? | Travel Resort Services. (2018, October 16). https://www.trsinc.com/why-vacations-are-important/#:~:text=Vacations%20increase%20productivity%20%E2%80%93%20Proven%20data

Waters, S. (2022, January 3). *10 ways to take time for yourself even with a hectic schedule.* Www.betterup.com. https://www.betterup.com/blog/take-time-for-yourself

Coach, H. D.-C. C. (2021, May 12). *23 Proven Journal Prompts to Unlock Your Career Change Success · Inner Resourcing.* Inner Resourcing. https://www.innerresourcing.co.uk/23-proven-journal-prompts-to-unlock-your-career-change-success/

. https://scatteredquotes.com/not-mountain-we-conquer/

140 Empowering Quotes about Money and Personal Finance. (2020, September 15). Marriage Kids & Money. https://marriagekidsandmoney.com/20-empowering-quotes-about-money-and-personal-finance/

Chen, J. (2021, March 23). *Money Management Definition.* Investopedia. https://www.investopedia.com/terms/m/moneymanagement.asp

The Importance of Money Management. (2019, May 21). Dechtman Wealth Management. https://dechtmanwealth.com/the-importance-of-money-management/

What Is a Checkbook? (n.d.). The Balance. Retrieved October 10, 2023, from https://www.thebalance.com/what-is-a-checkbook-5220492

7 Reasons to Balance Your Checkbook. (2012, September 21). Savingsaccounts. https://www.savingsaccounts.com/articles/reasons-to-balance-your-checkbook

budgeting, F. B. F. L. M. C. has been writing about, University-Idaho, personal finance basics since 2005 S. teaches writing as an online instructor with B. Y., Cary, is also a teacher for public school students in, & Caldwell, N. C. R. T. B. editorial policies M. (n.d.). *7 Reasons Balancing Your Checking Account Is Important.* The Balance. https://www.thebalance.com/how-to-balance-your-bank-accounts-each-month-4105885

8 Simple Steps for Balancing your Checkbook - Marquette Bank. (n.d.). Emarquettebank.com. https://emarquettebank.com/financial-education/articles-insights-for-you/eight-simple-steps-for-balancing-your-checkbook

Birken, E. G. (2020, July 13). *How To Balance A Checkbook In A Paperless World*. Forbes Advisor. https://www.forbes.com/advisor/banking/how-to-balance-a-checkbook/

(2023). Macu.com. https://www.macu.com/must-reads/checking/guide-to-managing-a-paperless-checking-account-fined

Natasha Munson: Money Emotions - Money Quotes DailyMoney Quotes Daily. https://itsamoneything.com/money/natasha-munson-money-emotions/

Schwahn, L. (2020, December 18). *What Is a Budget?* NerdWallet. https://www.nerdwallet.com/article/finance/what-is-a-budget

What Is a Budget? (n.d.). Ramsey Solutions. https://www.ramseysolutions.com/budgeting/what-is-a-budget

What Is Zero-Based Budgeting? (n.d.). NerdWallet. https://www.nerdwallet.com/article/finance/zero-based-budgeting-explained#:~:text=Zero%2Dbased%20budgeting%20is%20a

Kagan, J. (2022, March 14). *Zero-Based Budgeting (ZBB)*. Investopedia. https://www.investopedia.com/terms/z/zbb.asp

What Is a Pay-Yourself-First Budget? (n.d.). The Balance. https://www.thebalance.com/the-pay-yourself-first-budgeting-method-453955

Dave Ramsey's Envelope System Explained. (n.d.). Ramsey Solutions. https://www.ramseysolutions.com/budgeting/envelope-system-explained

How to Budget Using The Envelope System. (n.d.). NerdWallet. https://www.nerdwallet.com/article/finance/envelope-system

Whiteside, E. (n.d.). *What Is the 50/20/30 Budget Rule?* Investopedia. https://www.investopedia.com/ask/answers/022916/what-502030-budget-rule.asp#:~:text=Senator%20Elizabeth%20Warren%20popularized%20the

Mint.com. (2020). 50/30/20 Budgeting Rule and How to Use It [YouTube Video]. In *YouTube*. https://www.youtube.com/watch?v=1oGIriVHxRA

Speigner, M. (2021, May 12). *The Genius "No Budget" Method to Manage Your Money Each Month*. Easy Budget. https://www.easybudgetblog.

com/the-genius-no-budget-method-to-manage-your-money-each-month/

The No-Budget Budget. (2012, October 22). MoneyCrush. https://www.moneycrush.com/the-no-budget-budget/

Kagan, J. (2019). *Credit Score.* Investopedia. https://www.investopedia.com/terms/c/credit_score.asp

Understanding Credit Scores - Experian. (2016, April 21). Www.experian.com. https://www.experian.com/blogs/ask-experian/credit-education/score-basics/understanding-credit-scores/

How do I establish credit? - Wells Fargo. (2019). Wellsfargo.com. https://www.wellsfargo.com/financial-education/basic-finances/build-the-future/cash-credit/establish-credit/

Tips to Establish Credit for the First Time. (n.d.). Capital One. https://www.capitalone.com/learn-grow/money-management/how-to-establish-credit/

Lake, R. (2022, January 2). *Want a Better Credit Score? Here's How to Get It.* Investopedia. https://www.investopedia.com/how-to-improve-your-credit-score-4590097

Ismat Mangla. (2019, May 30). *How to Improve Your Credit Score Fast.* Experian.com. https://www.experian.com/blogs/ask-experian/credit-education/improving-credit/improve-credit-score/

11 Things to Know Before Getting Your First Credit Card. (n.d.). NerdWallet. https://www.nerdwallet.com/article/credit-cards/things-to-know-first-credit-card

(n.d.). https://money.usnews.com/credit-cards/articles/what-you-should-know-before-getting-your-first-credit-card

The 8 Cardinal Rules of Using a Credit Card. (2019, August 27). The Motley Fool. https://www.fool.com/the-ascent/credit-cards/articles/the-8-cardinal-rules-of-using-a-credit-card/

Smith, M. (2014, June 28). *10 Rules Of Using Credit Cards You Must Know.* Lifehack. https://www.lifehack.org/articles/money/10-rules-using-credit-cards-must-know.html

Black, M. (2023, April 24). *How To Get A Personal Loan.* Bankrate. https://www.bankrate.com/loans/personal-loans/how-to-get-personal-loan/

Diver, C. (2019, June 13). *How to apply for a personal loan.* Intuit Credit

Karma. https://www.creditkarma.com/personal-loans/i/how-to-apply-for-a-personal-loan

CFA, G. M. (n.d.). *Interest Rates: What They Are And How They Work*. Bankrate. https://www.bankrate.com/personal-finance/what-are-interest-rates-and-how-do-they-work/

Kasasa. (n.d.). *5 Things To Know About Car Loans Before Applying*. Www.kasasa.com. https://www.kasasa.com/blog/auto-loans/car-loan-facts

Top Things You Should Know When Buying a Car. (2019). Bank of America. https://www.bankofamerica.com/auto-loans/what-to-know-when-buying-car/

Stammers, R. (n.d.). *Financing Basics For First-Time Homebuyers*. Investopedia. https://www.investopedia.com/articles/mortgages-real-estate/08/homebuyer-financing-option.asp

What To Do Before Applying For A Mortgage. (n.d.). Www.quickenloans.com. Retrieved October 10, 2023, from https://www.quickenloans.com/blog/top-7-applying-home-loan

SHORT QUOTES: There are many things in life that will catch your eye, but only a few will catch your heart ... pursue those.. http://www.theshortquote.net/2012/04/sight-vs-insight-eye-vs-heart-choose.html

Top Reasons to start Investing at an early age - Axis Bank. (n.d.). Www.axisbank.com. https://www.axisbank.com/progress-with-us/invest/top-reasons-to-start-investing-at-an-early-age

Investing Guide for Teens (and Parents). (n.d.). The Balance. https://www.thebalance.com/investing-guide-for-teens-and-parents-4588018#:~:text=Some%20of%20the%20best%20investments

Connick, W. (2017, November 2). *Your Teenager Should Have a Retirement Account. Here's Why.* The Motley Fool. https://www.fool.com/retirement/2017/11/02/your-teenager-should-have-a-retirement-account-her.aspx

Fernando, J. (2021, December 5). *What is a 401(k) Plan?* Investopedia. https://www.investopedia.com/terms/1/401kplan.asp

Why 401K plans are so great. (n.d.). Icon. https://www.iconsavingsplan.com/the-basics/start-saving/why-401k-plans-are-so-great/#:~:text=One%20of%20the%20most%20powerful

Traditional IRA Definition, Rules and Options. (n.d.). NerdWallet. https://
www.nerdwallet.com/article/investing/ira/what-is-a-traditional-
ira#:~:text=A%20traditional%20IRA%20is%20a

Jones, M. (2021, June 2). *Roth IRA: What It Is, How It Works & How To Start
One | Seeking Alpha.* Seekingalpha.com. https://seekingalpha.com/arti
cle/4432577-what-is-a-roth-ira?external=true&gclid=CjwKCAi
A4KaRBhBdEiwAZi1zzu8BgT6Ep18XBaVis-
QMlwXT6PB_zQPoEHKBSrcLd6SwuoT7wEAhJxoC8w4QAv
D_BwE&utm_campaign=14049528666&utm_medium=cpc&utm_
source=google&utm_term=132628631894%5Edsa-
1635534203249%5E%5E584965509582%5E%5E%5Eg

Simplified Employee Pension (SEP) Definition. (2019). Investopedia. https://
www.investopedia.com/terms/s/sep.asp

What is a Roth Conversion, and how does it work? (2023). https://www.
annuityexpertadvice.com/roth-conversion/